NEVER ENOUGH

A NAVY SEAL COMMANDER
ON LIVING A LIFE OF
EXCELLENCE, AGILITY, AND MEANING

MIKE HAYES

CELADON
BOOKS

NEVER ENOUGH. Copyright © 2021 by Michael Hayes. All rights reserved. Printed in the United States of America. For information, address Celadon Books, a Division of Macmillan Publishers, 120 Broadway, New York, NY 10271.

www.celadonbooks.com

The Library of Congress Cataloging-in-Publication Data is available upon request.
ISBN 978-1-250-75337-3 (hardcover)
ISBN 978-1-250-75336-6 (ebook)

Our books may be purchased in bulk for promotional, educational, or business use. Please contact your local bookseller or the Macmillan Corporate and Premium Sales Department at 1-800-221-7945, extension 5442, or by email at MacmillanSpecialMarkets@macmillan.com.

First Edition: 2021

10 9 8 7 6 5 4

This book is dedicated to my soulmate, Ni,
who has been my rock and inspiration for more than twenty-five
years. Here's to our next fifty years, and beyond.

CONTENTS

SECTION THREE: NEVER MEANINGFUL ENOUGH

AUTHOR'S NOTE

As you'll learn in these pages, being a SEAL means living a life of service and placing others before self. These principles drive everything I do. I resisted writing this book for years, feeling strongly about never profiting from my service to this nation or from the SEAL name. In that spirit, I founded the 1162 Foundation, a 501(c)(3) organization, named after the date President Kennedy commissioned the SEALs—January 1, 1962—in order to help address the critical needs of families in the special operations community who have lost their heroic loved ones and spend every day trying to survive the best they can. Like every SEAL of my era, I've lost so many incredible teammates, each of whom left behind equally incredible family members who were forced to find a way forward through loss as a result. At the time of this writing, several mortgages for Gold Star widows have already been paid off due to my efforts and the generosity of others. My primary intention in writing this book is to generate revenue to help many, many more families. To that end, I have pledged to donate a minimum of $250,000 from my royalty earnings from this book to the 1162 Foundation with the explicit goal of helping these Gold Star families. With your help, we can grow that number and do tremendous good in the world. This book is intended to share, teach, and inspire—and, in the process, raise awareness of veterans' issues and provide help to these families, who are in such need. It is my privilege to offer my lessons and stories, in the hope that it will help you find even just a bit more meaning and purpose in your own life. Together, we can help the brave families who have answered our nation's highest call.

INTRODUCTION

It was 2007 in Fallujah, Iraq. Three o'clock in the morning, out in the streets. Darkness, dust, misery, dehydration. Potential danger coming from every direction. My Navy SEAL Team was on an operation to find a particular set of bad guys, and we had brought ourselves to a house where we had learned they might be hiding. Most of the team had entered the house, and I was one of a few SEALs outside, providing "command and control" for our teammates inside.

Suddenly, an Iraqi man wearing a traditional long white robe stepped out of a neighboring house. He reached quickly into his outfit, his hand disappearing from view—and this is the moment a life-or-death decision had to be made.

+ + +

I'll jump to the ending of that story. The man was pulling an ID card from his pocket. He was an innocent bystander who happened to be in a dangerous place and unwisely reached for something in his robe. Fortunately, my team had the confidence to wait a fraction of a moment, to assess the potential threat and think about the bigger picture before reacting.

Was this man in fact a deadly threat? Maybe, but we weren't sure. Did we have to shoot yet, or did we have time? Well, as it turns out, we did have just a little bit of time—to get more information, to watch his face, his eyes, to watch his hand as it emerged from his robe. We were aimed and ready—even if he had a weapon, he would have still needed to pull it from his robe, point it at us, and pull the trigger. It wasn't going to be minutes, or even seconds, but my teammates had the confidence in their ability to know they could wait until they saw just a little more.

Because we also knew the risks. Shooting innocent civilians doesn't help us win the support of the people, it doesn't help us find an ultimate path to victory, and regardless of the strategic implications, this was still a man's life.

+ + +

It sounds, at first, like a simple enough story—innocent man not killed by SEAL Team—but it's easy to imagine things turning out very differently. And it may sound unrelatable, if you've never been on the battlefield, but the reality is that each of us makes these kinds of decisions—to take action, or not—all the time, with varying stakes, and with varying time pressures. Should you take on a new project, or lower the risk of failure by sticking with something you're already comfortable with? Commit to growth within your organization, or jump to a different one, hoping it'll accelerate your career path? Reach out to a friend in need, or decide you just don't have the time?

I've spent my career trying to figure out how to make these kinds of choices most effectively, learning from the most successful people around me how to approach the world and our fellow citizens in order to live a life of the highest meaning, mission, and value. We get better, I've certainly found, by reflecting on what we've done and listening to the journeys of others.

As for me, I've lived a lifetime of once-in-a-lifetime experiences. I've been held at gunpoint in Peru and threatened with execution. I've jumped out of a building rigged to explode in Iraq. I've helped amputate a teammate's leg in Afghanistan. I've made countless life-ending decisions to drop bombs on our country's enemies—and sometimes I've made those decisions in mere seconds. I've made calls to parents that no parent ever wants to receive, and I've written hundreds of emails to my wife and daughter telling them how much I love them, just in case those were the last words of mine they'd ever read. I've prayed my men would survive every day—and I've made the decisions to help make that happen.

I've also run hundreds of meetings in the White House Situation Room. I led the process to create a new strategic arms treaty with the Russians, and went to Moscow for negotiations. I've developed sensitive corporate strategy and been responsible for countless multimillion-dollar deals.

In sum, I've spent the past twenty-five years feeling extraordinarily lucky to have the privilege to serve this country in a variety of ways—from my very first days in SEAL training as a twenty-one-year-old to my service as a Navy SEAL Commander in Afghanistan, as a White House Fellow and Director of Defense Policy and Strategy at the National Security Council under Presidents George W. Bush and Barack Obama, and in the boardrooms of public and private multibillion-dollar companies—and through it all, I've found that the most successful, satisfied, fulfilled people around me have always strived to contribute more, and pushed themselves to do as much as they can across whatever dimensions are most important to them, wherever they believe they can make the most difference.

This continuous striving to make a bigger difference—for yourself, for your organization, or for the world—is what I believe holds the key to great outcomes in almost any situation, and it's the mindset I'm talking about when I say "Never Enough." It's this push to realize that the goal shouldn't be to do just enough to get by, but to always look for more ways to make an impact.

I talk about "Never Enough," and sometimes people get the idea that I'm pushing for perfection, for someone to never be able to feel proud of what they've accomplished or satisfied that they've done the best they can do. But that's not it at all. "Never Enough" is about understanding that whatever you're striving to accomplish—whether that's becoming a SEAL, excelling in your current profession, or making a difference in the lives of the people in your family or community—you can always grow your capacity, increase your knowledge and skills, and invest more in the people and causes around you. It's not just so that next time you take on a challenge, your best can be even better, but so you can push yourself to truly align your actions with the goals you're trying to achieve.

We can never be present enough, purposeful enough, and thoughtful enough as we approach each day. We can do the hard thinking that helps us truly understand what motivates us, and what kind of life we're hoping to live—and then we can harness our energy to get us closer to those goals. It's about acting with intention rather than letting life carry us along on a trajectory we don't control. It's about considering our mission at every step along the way. It's about aiming for excellence, agility, and meaning in everything we do and not being complacent and just giving up. We won't all be SEALs, but we all have aspirations and dreams, and we can all improve the lives of our friends and colleagues, the organizations we choose to be part of, and the world. It's never enough to give up trying to achieve the things that matter most to each of us—and that's where this book aims to help.

+ + +

I remember early on in SEAL training—a grueling experience where out of my starting class of 120, just 19 ended up graduating as SEALs—when we had to run 2 miles in soft sand, wearing boots and long pants in hundred-degree summer heat. We sprinted as hard as humanly possible for more than 10 minutes, then reached even deeper when the finish line was in sight. The instructors immediately pounced on us, saying we were the worst class they'd ever seen in SEAL training, and forced us to do the entire run again—but faster. Some of us improved our speed the second time around, finding reserves we didn't know we had, and some of us just couldn't. The instructors separated us into two groups and told those of us whose speed had improved that we were failures, because the faster speed meant we hadn't truly given it our all the first time around. They told the group whose speed had declined that they didn't dig deep enough the second time and that clearly they didn't know what it meant to be a SEAL. The instructors wanted all of us to understand that every run had to be our best run, and that the minimum was never good enough.

I realize now that whether we improved that second time or not wasn't the point. We can't always control our outcomes. Instead, the point was that no matter what came before, we can't stop pushing. We can't give up. High-performing people inevitably live in two places at once. We do our absolute best, and we also realize that our best is a moving target. No one is perfect, and no situation is perfect, either. There will always be distractions, obstacles, limits, and emotions that get in the way. Sometimes we'll fall short, but that doesn't mean we stop trying. Sometimes we'll succeed, but that doesn't mean we're finished. We can always grow our capacity, make ourselves more likely to hit our targets, conquer potential stumbling blocks, and expand the impact of what we do. I tell people all the time that I'm not afraid of aiming high and missing—I'm afraid of aiming low and hitting.

We have to aim the highest we can, and when we hit that goal, aim higher—or think about whether we ought to have a different goal entirely. We can celebrate success, but also realize that our journey is never finished. We can achieve greatness, but also understand that to truly fulfill our most important missions in life, the road never ends. While we can and certainly should be proud of what we've done up until now, it is ultimately never enough. That's the mindset I believe can drive us all to lead more complete, more rewarding lives, each making the world a better place in our own unique way. That's the mindset I want to share in this book, arming you with stories and lessons to inspire you to do your best, be your best, and achieve the most you can possibly achieve.

✦ ✦ ✦

Another story from the battlefield, to help attach some concrete ideas to the goals of this book: For years in Afghanistan, our mission as a nation and our path to success were unclear. "Nations are really good at starting wars and really bad at ending them," I once told the *Wall Street Journal*. When I took over as Commander of our SEAL Team in southeast Afghanistan, I realized the best path forward wasn't just to fight the Taliban, but to reach out to them as people, to reinvigorate a reconciliation program that we hadn't been able to get off the ground, and to appeal to our enemies with compelling reasons to give up their weapons and join us for peace.

My team and I approached groups of Afghan fighters—not without risk, of course—and I gave talks and drank gallons of tea in Taliban-infested villages, directly and indirectly telling fundamentalists committed to the destruction of both America and the government of Afghanistan that maybe we weren't so different from each other. I'm a tribal leader, I said, just like you are, and our tribes have been killing each other for over a decade. We want peace, I explained, and we truly want you to participate in your own government, next to the great and innocent civilians in your country. If you are interested in having that conversation, in helping us both reach that common goal, I told them, here is the cell phone number of my interpreter.

We tried to understand their motivations, which, to a great extent, were economic. They needed money, and they needed infrastructure in their villages. They needed a channel and they needed a voice. We offered them three-month stipends, jobs protecting their villages, development projects like well-digging and school-building, and subsequently an opportunity to have a voice in how to help govern and care for their peace-loving fellow citizens.

The efforts began to pay off. We got calls and overtures from Taliban leaders, and we got fighters to come out of the hills and give up their black Taliban head wraps in exchange for the benefits we had offered. Over ten months, my team and I influenced over a hundred Taliban fighters to rejoin their government and people. It was not because anything about the war had fundamentally changed, nor was it because we were threatening them with powerful people and weapons. It was because we tried to understand their motivations, and tried to find common ground; we looked at the big picture and tried to take real action that would get everyone closer to their goals. We tried to think about a model we could scale, and that would build toward true and lasting success and peace.

Continuing our typical course may have been good enough for me to keep my job and good enough to keep the situation in Afghanistan from getting worse, but it wasn't going to make the biggest difference. There was more we could do, more we needed to do. The status quo simply wasn't enough, and really, if you dug a little deeper, there were three critical levels at which one might say it wasn't enough:

First, it wasn't *excellent* enough—we weren't always working hard enough to understand the needs of our Taliban enemies, to understand their point of view and their situation. Second, we weren't *agile* enough—we didn't have the absolute best systems in place to address their needs, and to help them in ways they would appreciate. And third, the work we were doing, while im-

Agile Enough and understand how to shift between roles to best serve our missions, how to put systems in place that lead to superior decision-making, and how to keep our teams as flexible and responsive as possible.

On an impact level, we must act to be *Never Meaningful Enough*, knowing what will make the biggest difference for the people in our lives and in our communities, and potentially on an even larger scale.

In the chapters that follow, I will explore different aspects of the headline principle, through stories and examples from my life and career, from the mistakes I've made and the lessons I've learned, and the change I've helped bring to the nation and the world.

Taken together, I believe this is how we become the best we can be, the people others rely on, and also the people who know how to rely on others in turn. This is how we do work of value, live lives of value, and stretch ourselves to reach our highest potential. This is how we can ultimately live in a nation of character, where leaders strive to be better, businesses strive to be better, and government strives to be better. This is how we pull people and organizations up. This is how we achieve our dreams.

Whether you are a college student, a young professional, a military servicemember, or an experienced leader within government or in the corporate world, we're all the same in so many more ways than we are different. We're all looking to live with more meaning and purpose, to succeed in our organizations, and to positively impact ourselves, our friends and colleagues, and others we may not even know. So many times in my life, I've seen the power of "Never Enough" come into play and lead people to improve not just their own circumstances, but the circumstances of those around them. It's a way of thinking that applies no matter your stage of life, no matter your level of organizational responsibility, and no matter your ultimate goals.

I talk sometimes about my grandmother's two sisters, who both became nuns in the Catholic Church and lived lives that were intensely meaningful to perhaps a few hundred or thousand people who benefited deeply from their work. On the other side of the continuum, there are people working on policy issues in Washington, DC, who might over the course of their careers move the needle a tiny percentage on some issue that can affect millions of lives in some small but significant way. There are parents whose largest goal in life is to go as deeply as they can in helping their children succeed and thrive—a narrow but hugely impactful focus on one, two, three people's paths in the world. And there are people running multibillion-dollar companies, touching colleagues and customers worldwide. These can all be deeply valuable, deeply meaningful pursuits, and there's no right or wrong in choosing to pursue any of them, no value judgments intended as I discuss the range of paths that people take in their lives.

No matter what journey you're on, my intent with this book is to help you figure out what's truly important, and then provide some ideas and skills to help get you there. In that spirit, I encourage you to reach out when you've finished this book and share your story—and to reach out to those around you to share any lessons my stories have helped you learn.

I remind my daughter each morning not to "have" a great day, but to "make it" a great day. "Have" is passive, implying that the world will simply happen around her, while "make" tells her to go out and cause things to happen, to actively create that great day for herself and others. You're already making this a great day by deciding to do the hard work of self-reflection, striving to learn and grow, staying agile and flexible, and looking for ways to push your values out into the universe. Together, we can make all our days greater—by being "Never Enough," and bringing enormous positive change to our lives and the world.

SECTION I

NEVER EXCELLENT ENOUGH

CHAPTER 1

CHOOSE THE HARD PATH

Excellence in Knowledge and Capacity

I was in Kosovo in 1999, in the middle of winter, leading a small surveillance team in the mountains just a few hundred meters from the Serbian border. Freezing-cold temperatures, the darkness of night, howling winds—and both Kosovar Serbian and Albanian armies somewhere in that same snowy terrain, weapons ready, looking for an enemy to fight. As we suffered through the elements, the sun soon to rise, we knew we needed to find a place to rest and hide for the daylight hours. From our vantage point halfway up the side of a mountain, struggling to maintain our balance on the steeply sloping ground, we could see a natural line of drift below—railroad tracks, a 10-foot-wide patch of flat ground, a path that would have called out to anyone as the comfortable place we should naturally set up camp. Of course we wanted to move down there. I remember a young guy on our team incredulous that we would even be out in this kind of weather. "Humans can't survive in this," he said. "It's miserable."

The temptation to head down toward the easier path and the more comfortable site was real, but if it was calling out to us, we knew it would be calling out to anyone who happened to be coming that way. Going down there would make us more visible, more vulnerable, and more likely to run into trouble. So we set up camp a couple hundred meters up the steeply angled slope, and sure enough, within an hour and just a short time before sunrise, what looked like the entire Albanian army marched straight down that natural line of drift. Had we been camped there, they would have found us for sure. Doing the uncomfortable, exhausting thing—the hard thing—saved us that day.

When I tell that story, I call it the "this sucks, let's stay here" lesson. It's not always so black and white, such a direct line you can draw between the choice to struggle and your ultimate success, but I've seen it time and time again. Doing the hard thing is how you win, how you grow, and how you end up getting the most out of life. If there's one principle that has shaped my career, it's this one, and that's why I felt it was the perfect place to start this book. Doing the hard thing, choosing the hard path, moving toward the most difficult challenges, aiming high—and trusting that you'll either succeed or you'll learn something, so either way it's a victory—got me to the SEALs, to the White House, and to senior roles in the private sector. It's the first thing I believe everyone ought to think about when approaching their life's trajectory. Am I letting myself follow the easy path, or am I moving up that mountain, looking for the difficult campsite that will give me the best chance to achieve my ultimate mission?

+ + +

Somehow I knew, even as an undergraduate at Holy Cross College, that there was value in chasing the hard path. It wasn't that I was a great student or had been born with some amazing leadership skills—I absolutely wasn't. But I did have determination, a solid work ethic, and a hero I looked up to. My grandfather graduated from the Naval Academy in 1940, and was nursing a hangover in a bungalow on the Pearl Harbor Naval Base the morning of December 7, 1941, when the Japanese began bombing. He was with seven others at the time, and when he heard that first wave of something going on, he knew he needed to get in his jeep and go toward the harbor, back to his ship. None of the others would go with him. They all believed they were safer where they were. He told me the scariest part was heading toward the ship, driving past a Marine guarding the gate at 45 miles an hour, without stopping, worrying the guard would shoot him.

My grandfather made it to his ship and manned his battle station. He was on board that ship for the third wave of attacks and tended to many wounded that day. In the wake of the bombing, he realized that he didn't want to spend his career on the ground or at sea. When he'd tell me this story, he would point up at the sky and say he wanted to be "up there." He put in a transfer to become a pilot, and after flight school, as World War II raged across the Pacific, he ended up stationed in the Aleutian Islands doing long-range bombing missions from the outermost islands and helping to attack strategic sites in northern Japan. He took over as the Commanding Officer of his thirty-five-plane bombing squadron at age twenty-six, after his own Commanding Officer was shot down, and he later served as a test pilot for the Navy's first helicopters and the Commanding Officer of the Navy's first helicopter squadron during the Korean War. He ended his career as a professor of Naval Science at Holy Cross and Commanding Officer of the school's ROTC training unit. He taught me about causes greater than self, what it means to serve, and how to keep pushing yourself to get better.

My grandfather didn't pressure me to follow his footsteps into the Navy, but he set an example of service and sacrifice that I've tried to live up to my entire life. I remember as a Holy Cross freshman going to a memorial service for a recent ROTC Navy SEAL graduate named John Connors, who had died in the US invasion of Panama in 1989. I learned what the SEAL community was that day, and what it meant to be part of it. John's selfless service, his push to contribute, and his impact on the world all made me want to be a SEAL. I had signed up for ROTC mostly because it was a path to paying for college. I initially figured I would put in my four years of obligatory service, maybe become a logistics officer or fill some other non-combat function, get out with a few years of great, meaningful experience, and go get an MBA. But the summer after my sophomore year, I had to do three weeks of service, aimed at helping me decide if I wanted to serve on a ship, on a submarine, as a pilot, or in some other typical Navy role. My group had one day of SEAL exposure, where everyone we met told us how hard it was to be a SEAL—and the more they talked about how hard it was, the more I became attracted to the challenge.

The next summer, I spent three weeks on what they called an aviation summer cruise. I got to fly an A-6 jet off the aircraft carrier USS *Saratoga*, explore the Spanish vacation island of Mallorca in my off-hours, and spend lots of time hanging out with adventurous pilots. I thought it was all some of the coolest stuff I'd ever done. And then I went to Coronado, California, for what was called Mini-BUD/S (Basic Underwater Demolition/SEAL Training). It was a one-week course designed to reduce attrition in the regular BUD/S program by exposing ROTC students to the rigors of what SEAL training was actually like, with the goal of keeping people from applying for the SEALs unless they were certain it was something they wanted and thought they could handle. The days were long. We were tested in the water and out of it: obstacle courses, grueling runs, endless swims. There would be only twelve ROTC students nationwide chosen to become SEAL officers, versus a few hundred slots for pilots.

During my senior year, and shortly before I had to choose whether to apply to become a pilot, a SEAL, or something else, Father Michael Ford sat next to me at a hockey game and changed the course of my life. Father Ford told me there had been a last-minute cancellation opening up a spot in his five-day silent retreat, the Spiritual Exercises of Saint Ignatius of Loyola, the founder of the Jesuits. It was a highly sought-after program, and Father Ford said he wanted me to attend. I tried to find a reason to say no, but I didn't have one. Instead of a week of winter vacation, I spent the time with twenty classmates in a retreat house on the ocean in Narragansett, Rhode Island. There was no speaking, just thinking, reading, contemplating, and reflecting.

At the time, my Naval "service selection" choice felt like a hard decision to make—pilot or SEAL?—but during the retreat, I realized that at the elemental level, there was a key difference: being a pilot is man against machine; being a SEAL is man against himself. As a pilot, you're an expert at one task. As a SEAL, you're doing something different all the time. You're exposed to every element of military work—and expected to have the agility to step into any role and instantly thrive. If being a pilot was like playing one instrument to perfection, being a SEAL was like conducting a band. (That's a theme that will show up again later in the book.) By the end of the five days, after prayer and reflection, it became clear to me: I wanted the challenge. I wanted to be a SEAL. In fact, by the end of the spiritual retreat, I was jumping into the freezing-cold water every day after my long afternoon run, just to start testing myself—knowing that SEAL training would be hard, I wanted to make sure I could handle the discomfort. I wanted to make sure I could do the hard things.

+ + +

Before we get too far into this book, I should tell you what it means to be a SEAL, for readers who may not know much about the organization. In some ways, the SEALs are similar to any high-performance organization. In other ways, of course, it's different—the stakes, every day, are about as high as they can be. Fundamentally, the SEALs are one of the world's preeminent special operations forces, tasked with knowing how to get anything done—from covert direct-action missions in the dark of night to working with local forces to improve security, governance, or infrastructure. We build bridges, open schools, and try to win the hearts and minds of local citizens. To sum it up, when you're faced with the hardest problems, you go to a SEAL. We're trained to be experts in getting to a desired outcome, and, in fact, figuring out multiple ways to get there. We pick the best risk-adjusted plan of attack, and then we execute. We're dynamic—we process information on the fly and change the plan as needed. We know how to put aside human discomfort and be hyperlogical, separate important information from noise, and dispassionately achieve our goals. At any given time, there are approximately 3,000 SEALs on active duty out of 1.2 million active military in the United States. There are four SEAL Teams on each coast—and I've been on all four of the East Coast teams (numbered 2, 4, 8, and 10) in my career. (I should also note that the SEALs were throughout my career an all-male force. The stories in this book are disproportionately about the men I served with because the majority of the stories are about the SEALs themselves. But I want to add that I also worked with many tremendously talented women during my service— lawyers, public affairs officers, communications and technology experts—without whom we could never have accomplished our missions.)

The SEALs are primarily a direct-action force. There are other incredible special operations forces or larger military units that do an amazing job working alongside or through locals to get tasks accomplished. The SEALs' main orientation is to do things ourselves. We pride ourselves on taking on the hardest missions needed for the good of the nation and then achieving success. The attrition rate through training is high—as I said in the introduction, my class of 120 was whittled down to 19 by graduation—but that's because the demands are intense. To survive, you need to be able to play many roles, and play them all well. You need to be able to excel physically, mentally, and emotionally. You need to execute on even the smallest details—and, at the same time, see the bigger picture and understand where you fit in the plan.

Being a SEAL—going through training, and then being out in the world helping to save lives and achieve your nation's strategic goals—you realize two things about excellence that define what I want to get across in this first chapter of the book: first, that the greatest trajectory to excellence is trying really hard things; and second, that the day you stop trying to improve is the day you stop being a SEAL. Every day, you need to maintain the state of mind that even the most excellent person can never decide that he or she is excellent enough.

We can take these two ideas and dive deeper into each one.

The Greatest Trajectory to Excellence Is Trying Really Hard Things

This was my epiphany during those five days of silence at Father Ford's retreat. If I wanted to be the best I could be, I needed to challenge myself with the greatest challenge there was. We are all faced with choices every day. There are always easier and harder paths in front of us. Do we look for the greater reward that carries with it more work, more risk, more uncertainty, and more chance for failure? Or do we aim for the smaller prize, limit our ambition, and play it safe? I've been convinced through everything I've seen in the world that in the long run, the path to success, meaning, and impact is the harder road to travel, every time. On the surface, sure, there is more opportunity to fail—but even in failure, we learn, and we use that knowledge to inform everything we do from that point on. Moving to the harder path and failing—but learning—is still a better outcome than doing what's easy and, even in success, not learning anything at all. If you don't keep learning, whether in success or failure, you don't grow. And if you don't grow, you'll never be able to tackle those harder hills.

SEAL training is all about moving to the harder path. We force young SEALs to conquer the hardest situations a human being can handle: timed 4-mile runs in soft sand while wearing full gear, including heavy boots; seven-man "boat crews," where you are forced as a team to carry a boat on your head everywhere you go for an entire day; "surf torture," where you are kept for hours in freezing ocean water, shivering and shaking, unsure when you will be allowed out; "drownproofing" exercises, where your hands and feet are tied and you need to survive in the pool for an hour without the use of your limbs; a 50-meter underwater swim that starts with an underwater somersault designed to disorient you and take away any forward momentum; and many more exercises just like that.

These drills are designed not just to be difficult, and not just to train SEALs to maintain their composure during the most challenging life-or-death situations, but to engender learning, growth, and the realization that you can do more than you think you can. Stick to easy tasks, and you'll never know how much you are capable of. We think we have certain limits, but if we don't stretch ourselves to test them, then we'll never know how much we can truly accomplish. That's why we must choose the hard path every time. It becomes a snowball effect: the confidence you gain from succeeding at something that seemed out of reach helps power you to even greater heights the next time. You learn that the only limitations are the negative thoughts in your head. You learn that you can do anything.

At the start of SEAL training, for instance, everyone is told that there will be a 5.5-nautical-mile swim by the end. That's a long swim, more than two hours at least. Hardly anyone when they arrive has ever done a swim that long before. It sounds nearly impossible. And then we work our way up to it, conquering physical challenges along the way that go well beyond that one, and by the time that nearly impossible swim comes up, it's not only easy—it's boring. One stroke after the next, and everyone makes it through.

"Okay," you might be thinking, "except I know that there are things I absolutely can't do, physically. I can't survive in the pool for an hour with my arms and legs tied. I just don't have the muscle strength." Let's put the physical challenges aside for a moment, because those, honestly, you can train for. The training may be hard, and the goal may seem out of reach, but we can all get stronger and stronger, better and better. And even if we ultimately can't survive in the pool for an hour with our arms and legs tied (and, please, don't try this without proper SEAL supervision!), we'll have gained so much from the training process. The truth is that often, the biggest obstacles preventing us from trying hard things aren't physical at all—they're mental. We don't want to be embarrassed. We don't want others to see us as failures. We care too much about what people will think.

I urge you to ask yourself, "What's the worst that can happen if I try this hard thing and fail?" Will your friends and family think less of you? If so, they shouldn't. Will the world think less of you? Will you not get the recognition you want or think you deserve? Well, you certainly won't get that recognition if you don't even try. Our fears are usually worse than the reality. Bad outcomes are usually not as bad as we imagine them to be. If we carefully walk our minds through the worst-case scenario of failure from whatever we're trying to do, we will usually realize that the stakes just aren't that high. The downside is insignificant compared to the upside of success. And yes, in the SEALs, the downside risks are sometimes tremendous—but we also take things step by step, and we make sure to only assume risk that is worth assuming. Most endeavors are not as high-stakes as SEAL missions, and the reality is that even in failure we learn, we get better, we clarify what challenges are most meaningful to us, and we put ourselves in a stronger position for success the next time we try something hard.

Which brings us to the second point . . .

The Day You Stop Improving Is the Day You Stop Being a SEAL

Or, really, it's the day you stop being excellent, because an excellent person is someone who knows they are never excellent enough, and that you have to keep striving, keep learning, and keep pushing. Choosing the hard path is only half the equation for success. You choose the hard path, and then you extract from those experiences all the lessons, all the growth, all the improvement you possibly can. We do have SEAL trainees who fail at tasks. We train to the point of failure—so we fail by design. Any future SEAL might stumble during a particular training event or exercise, and the organization knows that. There is almost always another chance to succeed. You stop, you think about what you did wrong, you think about what you could do better, and you try again. In the end, you might still fail, absolutely. And perhaps, at a certain point, you realize the SEALs may not be for you. But then you know you've pushed yourself to your limit, and you've learned something valuable: there are other journeys you may be better suited for, other places in this world where you can have an even bigger impact, more tailored to your strengths, your gifts, and your passions.

Sometimes you do succeed. During the last five weeks of training (held on an isolated island where it was said that no one could hear us scream), SEAL trainees are forced to do a certain number of pull-ups before every meal, or we're not allowed to eat in the dining hall. Instead, we're forced to run down to the water, jump in, and sit in the surf zone—alone, or with anyone else who has failed to perform—while a buddy brings over a tray of food and we eat, soaking wet. The first of those weeks, it was 12 pull-ups, then 14, 16, 18, and finally 20. Pull-ups were my weakest physical ability, by far. Even in my initial test to be admitted to SEAL training, I was only able to do 14, while some of my peers did 50. Each week, I was right at my limit and didn't think I could do even one more pull-up. But I worked as hard as I could, pushing myself every time I mounted the bar, and— with the exception of one meal, on my twenty-second birthday, where I ended up eating alone, soaking wet, smiling and laughing, trying to reframe it in my mind and think of it as a birthday present to myself—I did it. I reached deep down inside and did the pull-ups I needed to do to be able to eat dry.

We have to strive to keep getting better, to realize that there is always more growth ahead. That realization is so critical, that quest for improvement driving people to far greater heights than any amount of raw talent alone ever can. Between a person with greater raw abilities and a person always looking to improve, I will choose the second every time, no question. Long-term success is about hunger, passion, drive, and determination. We are limited only by our imagination and our work ethic. The decision isn't whether we can do something, but whether we are willing to put in the work it will take and make the necessary sacrifices.

You can be talented without having that drive to succeed, without being willing to do the work and stretch yourself. When I meet trainees with talent but insufficient hunger, I know they're going to fail. If you tell me that you're 99 percent sure you'll make it through SEAL training, I'm 100 percent sure you won't. You have to believe, you have to want it so badly, you can't allow even that 1 percent doubt to creep in. You have to know that you'll do whatever is required.

I've found that the hungriest people will, in fact, do whatever it takes, and they'll also get better and better along the way. The growth that gets us to be more and more excellent over time is powered by hard work, absolutely, but it's also powered by reflection and real learning. I can't emphasize this next point enough: the way to extract maximum knowledge from these hard challenges we undertake is to be truly objective and reflective about our performance, in success just as much as in failure. The way to get better over time is to know where we aren't good enough, what aspects of our life are not satisfying enough, which goals we're chasing aren't the right ones. This isn't always easy to internalize. We all have a natural tendency to want to focus on the positive, not dwell on what we could have done better. Especially when the result is good, we don't always want to rehash the mistakes we made along the way. And yet those are the mistakes that might lead to a poorer outcome next time, when the circumstances may be a little bit different.

In the SEALs, after every single mission we spend time running through what didn't go well enough. Even if things seemed to turn out perfectly, there are always places to improve, issues that can too easily be papered over until it's too late. We don't spend a lot of time talking about what went right. If something went well, it will likely go well again. The highest return on investment in conversations like these is achieved when we discuss in an honest and direct way what we could have done better. True, honest, and specific feedback is how we improve.

I should refine that just a bit. True, honest, specific, and *shared* feedback is how we improve. We debrief as a group because we can all learn lessons from each other, and because the leader of a group isn't the only one whose ideas and opinions matter. We also want to get all our thoughts on the table instead of splintering our team with backchannel discussions and private finger-pointing. When I worked in the White House, I was responsible for running the process to get a group of interagency experts to agree on a proposed draft version of a nuclear treaty with the Russians. I'll draw more lessons from this experience in later chapters, but relevant here is that after our first meeting, I received emails and calls from several stakeholders with complaints about other people in the room, sidebar information they thought I ought to know, whispers and secrets that kept us from having honest, productive conversations in the room.

I knew this was no way to get to a good outcome. At the beginning of the very next meeting, I stood at my spot at the head of the table and announced that if there was something worth saying, it should be said to the group. We have to own our opinions and be honest with each other, or we'll never have trust and we'll never reach the best outcome. Even if things are uncomfortable to share, you have to find a way to say them—it's the only way to get better.

+ + +

Hopefully, you're with me so far. Choose the hard path, and keep striving to improve. An excellent person is never excellent enough—true excellence comes from the continued striving. Reflective and objective feedback is critical. But I talk about choosing the hardest opportunities, and I talk about never losing that hunger to get better, never being too confident in what you already know, and I realize there are some traps that are easy to fall into while taking that advice. Three big traps, in fact, which I'll spend the rest of this chapter explaining how to avoid.

The L in SEAL Stands for "Lazy"

Or the longer version of this point: Choosing the hard path doesn't mean working hard simply for the sake of working hard. As SEALs, we focus on outcomes, not outputs. In the military—and certainly outside it—it's easy to get caught up in thinking about production. How many reports have you written? How many tasks have you completed? How many emails have you sent? None of it matters. The size of the effort ultimately doesn't count; our long list of tasks keeps us busy but doesn't actually get us closer to the goal. We don't get points for how many hours we studied for the exam, how much activity we generated, how many items were on our to-do list, or how many boxes we checked. We get credit for how many questions we got right.

It's easy in so many contexts to think about the journey and not the destination, to measure what we do instead of the outcome it leads to. But I'd rather my SEALs find the fastest path to the goal and save the rest of their time and energy for something else. Do it efficiently, achieve the desired outcome, and then move on. Life is either work or leisure. Get the work done, and then you have a valuable option: choose more work or enjoy more leisure. The hardest path doesn't always mean the longest hours—at least not if you're smart about it.

And it definitely doesn't mean pointless busy work. Heck, in SEAL training, one of my instructors had us do a thousand sit-ups. It's not that any of us couldn't do a thousand sit-ups, but if you're going to do a thousand sit-ups, you can be smart about it. When the instructors are watching, give them the perfect sit-up. But if no one's looking and sit-up number 712 is a little sloppy, and maybe really only half a sit-up, keep the bigger-picture goal in mind—even a thousand half sit-ups is a pretty good workout. There is power in conserving energy and focusing on the end result.

Doing Hard Things Is Not the Same as Doing Risky Things

Scaling a mountain without a harness is hard. It's also stupid. In the SEALs, every operation has risk. As I've mentioned already, we only want to take on risk that's worth assuming. In my very first deployment as a SEAL, I was in El Salvador, in charge of a seven-man SEAL squad. We were doing demolition training with our El Salvadoran counterparts, the FOEs (Fuerzas de Operaciones Especiales), the country's most elite special forces unit. We were alone in the jungle, blowing things up, no one in sight, and we decided to put together a larger fireball charge than any of us had ever made before—an explosion, a huge one, because we were twenty-something-year-old kids with piles of explosives and gasoline, and there didn't seem to be any danger in doing so. We poured 45 gallons of fuel into a 55-gallon drum, added the necessary steel wool and the C-4, or plastic explosives, and found a safe place to watch at a distance, with plenty of time until the resulting explosion.

And then, as the seven-minute fuse burned down, we saw a small South American aircraft come out of absolutely nowhere, at most a hundred feet in the air, puttering along, directly toward where our fireball charge was set to detonate. We looked at each other in total disbelief, then we looked at our demolition site, a couple hundred meters away from us. We knew we didn't have time to run back and disable the explosive without putting ourselves at huge risk, so there was nothing we could do but wait and hope. There we were, watching this plane unknowingly fly right into the danger zone and thinking we were about to witness a terrible disaster.

Our fireball charge exploded right on cue, sending a huge plume of smoke into the air. As the smoke cleared, we saw the plane, still puttering along—it flew just over our fireball, and fortunately, while I'm sure we gave the pilot quite a scare, there were no horrendous consequences.

My team and I learned a huge lesson: Not all risks are obvious. Sometimes there are dangers you won't anticipate. You need to train yourself to expect the unexpected, and no matter your motives, only take on risk that is worth taking on. We didn't need to detonate an explosive quite so large in order to get the same benefit from our training. We didn't have a strategic reason for doing so, and we created a risk we didn't need to create. That early-career scare has stuck with me ever since.

Another story, again from my time as a brand-new SEAL: The Navy needed four of us to help test some new equipment, and I was "volun-told" to take part in the exercise. They took us in a boat, two or three miles offshore, dropped us in the water, and told us to swim to the beach, stay for a few minutes, and then swim back to the boat together. It turned out that conditions were unexpectedly harsh—40-knot winds, nearly 8-foot-high waves—and the four of us immediately lost each other, unable to see more than a few feet in front of us. I swam for what felt like hours before I finally got to the beach . . . and once I was there, I could not see my teammates. I waited, and waited, but there was simply no sign of them. I figured maybe I had missed them, maybe I'd gotten slowed down by the waves, maybe they'd already made their way back. So I got back in the water and tried to return to the boat, even though I couldn't see it. In my mind, I had to complete the assigned mission at all costs, just keep going—this is what a SEAL has to do.

I couldn't find my way back to the boat. Because of the harsh conditions, I was using my Silva Ranger compass to do my best to swim a straight line of bearing to the planned link-up point. But it didn't work. I realized I must have drifted much more than I expected. I couldn't see back to the beach, either. For a few hours, I was basically lost at sea, worrying the three other (more experienced) SEALs would think I was a total screw-up. I had broken a fin strap, and at one point, I was startled (okay, scared) when I was moved about 10 feet in the water, bumped hard by a massive sea mammal. I imagined that no one would ever find my body, and everyone in the SEALs would think I must not have been a good swimmer—despite entering BUD/S training with one of the fastest swim times in the history of the program, and, along with my swim buddy, Chris Cassidy, coming seconds away from the fastest-ever 2-mile timed swim in BUD/S (you'll hear more about Chris in chapter 2).

Finally, the boat found me and picked me up, and I was quickly excoriated for being stupid enough to make the swim back out to sea. My three teammates had ended up down the beach from where the current had taken me—just a bit too far away for me to see them—and they stayed on the beach until the boat came for them, knowing conditions were too miserable to even attempt to head back. I had put myself at risk—for a training exercise!—because I confused doing the hard thing with doing the right thing. My decision was far too risky to make sense, even as a confident and capable swimmer.

For me, in that moment, the harder thing would have been to admit that trying to swim back to the boat was ridiculous. Changing the plan based on severely harsh conditions was the harder choice that I should have made, instead of taking a silly and unnecessary risk just to prove that I was a good, obedient "new guy."

There's a version of that story where I could blame my team for letting me down, the boat for not being at the right pickup point, or the trainers for not creating a better contingency plan for bad weather. But when I look back on it, the truer telling of that story is that nearly being lost (or eaten!) at sea drove me not to blame anyone for what could have happened, but to figure out what I needed to learn so that it would never happen again. And what I needed to learn was humility and risk assessment.

Sometimes the Hardest Thing Is Sticking to Your Values and Beliefs

Choosing the hard path certainly isn't always physical, and isn't always about the amount of effort or time something will take. In fact, I think the hardest choices we make are often the ones that involve going out on a limb, bucking conventional wisdom, or standing up to people in positions of authority when they're telling you something you simply don't believe. People generally don't get in trouble for following the rules—but when the rules conflict with what you know is right, whether in a moral sense ("We shouldn't treat people that way") or a practical sense ("There's a better way to make that paper clip"), sometimes the hard choice you need to make is to follow your instincts and accept whatever consequences might result.

In the SEALs, we're taught that if you think your mission has been compromised, you exfiltrate—you get out. That may mean canceling an entire mission, setting weeks of work—and ego—aside and saying you just can't take the risk involved with trying to accomplish what you've set out to do. In that case you need to go back to safety, come up with a new plan, and start again.

In 1997, I was in Kosovo on a reconnaissance mission to help enforce the Dayton Accords, the peace agreement ending the war in Bosnia between the ethnic Albanians and the Serbs who jointly occupied Kosovo. It was the very beginning of high-tech surveillance, where we had night-vision cameras for the first time and satellite radios to send near real-time images back to headquarters. These were huge breakthroughs at the time, cutting-edge technology. For these particular missions, we would go out in the field in groups of six—two two-person "observation posts" and one two-person "command post," the observation guys pushing into the dangerous areas to keep their eyes on the target and the command guys hanging back, placed centrally between the observation posts but out of the immediate danger zone, communicating via radio. I was at the command post with Jimmy G, our radio guy, and we were talking to our observation guys (Tom and Allan on one team, Chad and Steve on the other), who had eyes on a house out of which there appeared to be a huge transfer of illegal arms between the Russian forces, who were part of the peacekeeping mission, and the Kosovar Serbian forces. This was in direct violation of the Dayton Accords, and a big deal at the time. Our guys got pictures, and I communicated what we were seeing back to headquarters. We called our Green Beret counterparts, who manned a nearby location, and asked them to come search the house for confirmatory evidence.

It's important to note that we were traveling very light, as would be expected for a reconnaissance mission like this. We were not planning on getting into a gunfight, and even though we were armed, this was not intended to be an offensive, direct-action mission. I was quite young in my career, at a level known as O3—a lieutenant—and taking orders from the Army Special Forces Major (an O4-level officer, my superior at the time) back at headquarters.

I suggested to the Major that we should come off the target immediately after the Green Berets left, because we would be compromised at that point—the Russians or the Kosovar Serbians would see that someone had been in the house, and they would know that someone out there was watching them. And they would quite predictably come looking for us, putting us in great danger, particularly since we weren't armed for such a situation.

The Major said no, that we should stay in the field for 48 hours and "Charlie-Mike," or continue mission, watching after the Army guys finished trying to gather evidence. I told him via radio that this broke SEAL doctrine, and reminded him of the adage I had learned from experienced SEALs before me: "If you think you've been compromised, assume you have, and ex-filtrate." I believed we absolutely needed to exfiltrate, but he dis-agreed, and said it was an order for us to stay in the field. What do you do when your boss gives you a bad direction? I canvassed my guys and stated my logic, and we all asked each other how strongly we felt about it. We knew that pushing back was the right thing to do, but we also didn't want to go down the road of disobeying an order and potentially facing consequences— unless following that order was something we truly felt was going to put us in clear danger. In all honesty, we didn't feel strongly enough about it. We didn't think it was anywhere close to a certainty that anyone would find us where we were, and we knew that the easier path would be to listen to the order and save our fight for another day. This was an error in judgment and, in retrospect, could have cost us our lives.

We stayed out there, hidden among the neat rows of ever-greens in a several-acre manicured forest that had been planted for firewood. (We cut, bent, and strategically placed extra branches to hide ourselves during the day.) And sure enough, not two hours after the Army forces checked out the house, our observation guys saw three Kosovar Serbians approach the building and realize that windows had been broken—and then figure out that someone had been watching them. Those three ran off quickly, presumably down to their village, and came back at first darkness with nineteen armed soldiers—our guys counted—who began hunting for us in the forest. Chad, one of our observation guys, communicated back to me, "We have two armed soldiers methodically working their way down the edge of the forest. They are likely to see us. We need to either pull back or shoot them."

"I'm behind you either way," I told Chad, trusting him to make the right call, "but if you shoot them, just know that it will be a massive situation, and we are greatly outnumbered." There was no easy answer. Shoot, and then everyone knows where we are. But pull back, and we're eyes off the target, we're not doing the mission we're there to do, and we're all at risk because we don't know where the enemy is.

Chad and Steve quickly decided to pull back. After they were certain these two armed men were gone, they came back to the command post with me and Jimmy, so now the four of us were together. All of a sudden, we heard shots ring out. The Kosovar Serbians had begun shooting, an attempt to get us to shoot back and reveal our location. They sprayed the tree line with maybe thirty to sixty rounds of sporadic machine-gun fire. Once the shooting settled down, we communicated to our other two observation guys out in the field, telling them to pull back to where we were so that all six of us could be together, do our best not to be discovered, and get picked up by our "Quick Reaction Force" vehicles, which were on standby a few kilometers away. During the hours that followed, as we tried to avoid a gunfight, we were actively hunted. I was twenty-six years old and in charge of the lives of five other men. At one point, I heard approaching footsteps—stealthy footsteps, a noise I knew well, because I was often the one making it, trying to place one foot at a time down on a forest floor without crunching a single dead leaf or breaking a single twig. I heard someone taking one step about every ten seconds. I aimed my rifle in his direction and eventually saw him—long before he could see me. I took the slack out of my trigger, just a hair away from firing, and held my aim dead center on him. He got as close as 6 feet from me as I watched him crouch, squint, scan, and hunt us. I just remember thinking, *No . . . no . . . no . . .* If he had seen me, I would have had to kill him. But he didn't, and I was relieved I wouldn't have to give away our position to all the other men hunting us. It could not have been closer.

Carefully, silently, slowly, we got out. The intelligence we had gathered was useful, for sure, helping us figure out that the Russians were colluding with the Kosovar Serbians, support we hadn't been aware of and didn't have proof of until that point. But it wasn't worth the risk to our lives. I should have stood up to the Major, done what I knew was right, and not accepted the unnecessary risk. The hardest thing in that situation would have been to disobey a direct order—but I chose the easier path. It was a mistake. (And as soon as shots were fired, I knew that the Major himself realized it was a mistake, although he never directly acknowledged it.)

Years later, in Afghanistan in 2012, I saw a similar pattern emerging. I canceled a 72-hour mission just 24 hours in because I felt we had been compromised. I looked back at what I wished had happened in 1997 and made the hard call to end that mission early, to avoid the unnecessary risk. The leader on the ground in Afghanistan tried to fight me to keep the mission going. He said they had the high ground and full visibility on the enemy, and that they were going to be able to execute if they did get into a gunfight. But I sent a helicopter and pulled his team from the mission anyway, and afterward I sat them down and explained my thinking. You could get the best intelligence, you could kill thirty dangerous Taliban fighters—but if our odds had just changed, if our 99 percent chance of success fell to 96 percent, or 92 percent, the added risk was too much to take on in this situation. It is not worth the extra risk to your lives, I said, or to the missions down the road you are yet to accomplish, and will never accomplish if you're wounded or dead. They thought the hard thing was completing the mission. I knew the hard thing was setting ego aside and canceling it.

+ + +

We do the hard things. We never stop learning. We're objective and reflective so that we can apply our lessons in the future and never make the same mistake twice. As you look at your own life, you may not always know what the hard path is. Do you stay in a frustrating job that may get you to your goal, or do you leave for a more satisfying position that may not have as much upside? Do you start that new business you've been dreaming about, or do you convince yourself that the risks are too great and the chance of failure too high to make it worth it? The hard path isn't always obvious—clearly, I didn't have the best sense of it when I was deciding whether to swim back from the beach during that training exercise, or whether to push back against my superior in Kosovo. But we learn over time, and with experience. Now, when faced with two paths, I often find myself asking an important question: Which path makes me more uncomfortable? You may think it's smart to shy away from discomfort, but that's not where this advice is heading. Discomfort is often the biggest key to growth, and it's what tells you if the road ahead is the right kind of hard, the kind that you should be pursuing. I absolutely felt uncomfortable when I was heading to Washington to serve as a White House Fellow, and even when I decided to write this book. But that's how I knew these were challenges worth tackling.

In the next chapter, we'll talk all about discomfort, and how building your capacity for withstanding difficult conditions is just as critical as building your knowledge by always trying to learn and grow. It's not enough to do the hard things—you have to embrace them, be comfortable with them, and build your capacity to never shy away from the right challenge.

CHAPTER 2

BUILD COMFORT WITH DISCOMFORT

Excellence in Strength and Control

Back in 1996, I was held at gunpoint by five armed assailants in Peru. I was in Lima with six other SEALs, working with the GOEs (Grupo de Operaciones Especiales), the SEALs' closest counterparts in Peru. My team and I were helping to train them as part of an exchange program between allied nations, one country's military forces helping out another's, and strengthening important strategic national relationships. We were all getting ready to head to Iquitos, a port city that serves as the gateway to the Amazon rain forest, for some more training deep in the jungle. While five SEALs from my "squad" flew out, I stayed back with my senior enlisted, Ken, for an extra day to attend scheduled discussions at the US embassy and tie up some loose ends. Ken and I went out to dinner—at Tony Roma's, an American chain restaurant with locations all over the world. I was driving us back to our hotel in our rented Toyota Land Cruiser, a more expensive vehicle than most of those we saw on the roads in Lima, when suddenly a police car pulled in front of us and stopped short while another pinned us in from the rear, trapping us between them.

Three men got out of the front car—uniformed police officers, it seemed, carrying rifles. Ken and I were unarmed—the embassy had a strict "no arms" policy for servicemembers going out in the city, and besides, we didn't expect we'd be in danger while having dinner as we wrapped up a training mission. In all honesty, Ken and I disagreed with the no-arms policy, but we also weren't planning on wandering around the dangerous parts of town—predictably, Tony Roma's was in a perfectly ordinary, tourist-friendly location—so we complied without issue and left our weapons behind.

And really, had we been armed, it only would have complicated the situation to come. When the men first got out of their car, we had no reason to think they were anything but police officers, so we certainly wouldn't have shot them. But then one of the men, finger on trigger, viciously jammed the muzzle of his rifle into my head—twice—leaving a permanent bump behind my ear. At that point, we knew: these certainly weren't legitimate officers, and we were being ambushed. Indeed, they had the three necessary ingredients for an ambush, a checklist that every BUD/S trainee learns: surprise, superior firepower, and violence of action. These were, I concluded, corrupt policemen at the very least, and quite possibly members of the Shining Path, a Peruvian terrorist organization.

The men searched us. Had we been carrying weapons, they would have been taken from us and, even worse, would have prevented us from being able to explain ourselves away as innocent Americans who posed no threat. As it was, they took our wallets and the small gold Saint Christopher pendant my wife (my fiancée, back then) had given me, its back containing an inscription: *Safe in my heart, always.*

Two of the men pushed me to the passenger seat of our vehicle and forced Ken into the back. They started to question us in rapid-fire Spanish: Who were we? Why were we there? Ken spoke and understood Spanish at a basic level, while I was fluent (Profesora Borland from Holy Cross would have been proud!), so I told them that if they needed him to do something, they should tell me and I would translate. This was strategic just as much as it was practical. As Ken and I communicated back and forth about their instructions, we passed extra information to each other in order to put together elements of a plan. We repeated to one another the phone number of the embassy switchboard, which I had memorized on my first day in the country, and we decided where to meet up if we became separated: "Point 1, Main Gate, Naval Base in Callao," we confirmed to each other over the course of the questioning.

We both stayed purposefully calm, with the goal of keeping our attackers calm, and creating the easiest situation for them to simply take our wallets, take the car, and let us go. I told them, in Spanish, that we were "economistas" at the US embassy, desk workers who were just out to dinner. I didn't want them to think we were important, worth capturing or hurting, or potentially dangerous to them. They interrogated us for an hour as they drove around the city, asking some gruesome questions, not the worst of which was whether we liked being tortured.

I stayed *tranquilo* and acted like this was a routine occurrence. I made them think that I knew the deal: they would win, and get the car, and we would get to go home. My biggest concern was that if they killed us, our bodies would never be found. No one would know we were missing, possibly for days. The rest of the team in Iquitos—remember, this was a time before cell phones and email were ubiquitous—would have assumed we had some more loose ends to tie up in Lima, or that we'd had flight issues, neither of which would have been out-of-the-ordinary complications to our schedule.

There were points at which I saw the opportunity to escape with my life. As we drove farther and they questioned me more, they let down their guard slightly—removing the gun from my head, aiming it down—to a point where I was confident I could have grabbed the weapon and killed at least one of them or, alternatively, bailed out of the vehicle and survived. Ken could have acted on his own as well—but our concern was for each other. Had I tried to escape, the danger to Ken would have been infinitely greater. They would have almost surely hurt or killed him if I made any unexpected moves. I could have saved myself—but I wasn't going to do it if it meant an increased chance that my teammate would be harmed.

As we drove around, I ran through all the possibilities, my brain feeling like a super-computer running in slow motion and overdrive at once. Ken and I used coded language to communicate to one another the landmarks we saw outside the window. If I'd been armed, and had they not taken the weapon away, I could have shot all of them—but the car would have crashed at high speed, potentially injuring or killing all of us, and we would have had to contend with the other armed enemies following in a car behind us. Of course, that didn't matter, because I wasn't armed, and neither was Ken.

Finally, the driver pulled into a darkened neighborhood and

parked the car. He told us both to get out. I wasn't sure if we were about to be executed. I knew this was my moment to live or die. Ken and I moved quickly to put distance between us and the weapons, and jumped behind a tree. The men, deciding not to pursue us, drove off with our car. They must have been convinced enough that we were neither a threat nor a prize, and so, fortunately, we were not worth either holding on to or murdering. I later heard that a similar incident happened just a night or two after our experience . . . unfortunately, that time, the victim ended up being killed by their captors, shot and left in the street. Were we lucky, or had we effectively remained in control, giving ourselves the best chance to ultimately go free?

I took away two lessons from that night. First, I proved to myself that I was the kind of person I hoped I was, the kind who would never leave my buddy at risk just to save myself, even if it cost me my own life. Second, I realized how important it is to control your emotions, to stay calm, and to understand that success isn't just about attacking and conquering the hardest intellectual or physical challenges—choose the hard path, absolutely, as I explained in chapter 1—but also about remaining steady and rational during the toughest emotional challenges. I didn't bail out of that vehicle and leave my friend to die. I stayed calm and focused on the mission over my own safety, and we both ended up escaping alive.

Those lessons one at a time.

We Are Who We Are at Our Worst

It's easy to show the best sides of ourselves in situations we are confident we can handle. It's far harder when we're pushed beyond our perceived limits. We are who we are at our worst. That's how you measure someone's character: you see how they respond not in the 99.9 percent of life when they're comfortable, but in the 0.1 percent when they're not. To be excellent, we need to be comfortable with discomfort. In the most stressful situations, we need to be able to behave with the same calm rationality as we do when things are easy. That's what SEAL training teaches, and what anyone looking to thrive in life absolutely has to aim for.

Most of the time, especially in our modern existence, we're in climate-controlled conditions, with temperatures between 68 and 72 degrees Fahrenheit, wearing dry and appropriate clothing, well-rested and well-fed, not in extreme physical pain or undergoing significant mental duress. In those settings, what excuse do we have to not be kind, thoughtful, rational, and decent? Seeing how someone acts when they're truly stressed in some way is a far better indicator of character. Some people think that those hard moments give them a good excuse to deviate from the highest moral and ethical standards, to mistreat others, to speak poorly about colleagues or friends, or to otherwise act illogically. Nothing could be further from the truth. When things are genuinely difficult—physically, intellectually, or emotionally—that's when you have the greatest opportunity to prove to others (and to yourself) what you are made of.

These are the kinds of situations that distinguish high-performing people, and we should all see these situations as opportunities to show our true colors, prove our value, and make a difference. These are our chances to excel beyond what others in the room may be capable of in those tense moments. We need to not just survive the worst—we need to embrace the worst, embrace the lessons these circumstances can teach us and the challenge to be the people others can count on, turn to, and trust even when the going gets tough.

+ + +

SEAL training is all about manufacturing these moments and making us comfortable with discomfort, forcing us to expect the unexpected, pushing our perceived breaking points to the limit, and showing us how much more we are able to handle than we sometimes imagine. We're forced to survive Hell Week, the hardest training there is in the US military, where we have to stay awake for five and a half straight days, 120-plus hours, pushed physically and mentally by our instructors, in motion almost the entire time, in and out of freezing-cold water, through obstacle courses, running, swimming, doing thousands of push-ups a day, building ourselves into a true team. We worked in our "boat crews" of seven, running everywhere with a boat on our seven heads, or holding telephone pole–size logs over our heads for what felt like forever, or paddling together to get beyond the surf zone (but usually getting dumped and thrashed by the waves).

Stretching us beyond what we think is possible is the goal of Hell Week, and what ultimately ends up preparing us for the actual challenges ahead of us in our careers. At its core, being a SEAL is not just about living at the edge of human misery, but about thriving and achieving success in those conditions.

In the non-SEAL world, there is still plenty we can each do to push our limits and make ourselves more comfortable with discomfort. It might be as simple as reading the sections of the newspaper we're never drawn to and trying to stretch the boundaries of our knowledge. It might be reaching out to a friend or colleague in a situation where we would otherwise feel embarrassed or self-conscious. It might be traveling to a part of the world we are unfamiliar with. It might be letting ourselves feel hunger, thirst, or the temperature extremes that we would normally shy away from or "fix" much sooner than we have to. When we're cold, or hungry, or tired, our bodies warn us in the spirit of self-preservation. But sometimes those warnings have been trained to come on too soon. We start to worry even before we feel the feelings, and the feelings sometimes aren't even indicative of our body's true needs. We scare ourselves out of trying new things and stretching our boundaries. We only learn that we can do more than we realize by actually doing the things that scare us or make us miserable. You'll never grow if you just stay comfortable.

+ + +

In some ways, this sounds like the "do hard things" lesson from chapter 1. But there's a different point here. It's not just about doing the hard things—it's about seeing the hard things as opportunities for us to be our best instead of letting ourselves get overwhelmed by stress and anxiety. In part, it's about trying to relax, believing in our own talents and abilities, and rising above the pressures of any given situation. But it's also about finding the hard things that are right for each of us as individuals.

I mentioned that my SEAL training class shrank from 120 to 19 by graduation; the truth is that there weren't that many people who couldn't hack it physically. There were some, of course. But if you got into SEAL training in the first place, there were minimums you had already shown you could reach, and there were screenings that would have already weeded you out if you didn't have the raw horsepower needed to succeed. The issue, far, far more often, was mental. Being a SEAL—being able to embrace misery of the hardest kind—ended up being too much for a lot of the members of my class. But that just meant the SEALs weren't the right "hard thing" for them to tackle. Many of them ended up becoming quite successful in other arenas. They just needed to find the role where at their worst, they could be just as assured, just as capable, and just as steady as they were at their best.

We Have Control Over Our Emotions, and Must Maintain That Control

This is the second lesson I learned in Peru, and it plays out in a few different ways. First, attitude is so important. You can't make me have a bad day. You can try, absolutely, but only I can make me have a bad day. And I've had bad days—the loss of far too many friends, teammates, people who were like brothers to me—but you choose whether to let those bad days spin you negatively or decide you can only control what you can control, and that you can use what you do control to impact the rest of the world in a positive way.

Chris Cassidy was my "swim buddy" throughout SEAL training. He is now a NASA astronaut and former chief of the Astronaut Office, and spent much of 2020 in space for the third time, aboard the International Space Station. One of our exercises during SEAL training was ocean lifesaving, where we had to "save" our "drowning" instructors in high surf and freezing waters. Mostly it was an excuse to force us into the bitterly cold ocean for hours. We'd had other ocean exercises where we were told to lock arms with the man next to us and just lie there. And then lie there some more. The shivering and full-body convulsions come quickly when you're that cold. People "jackhammer" uncontrollably and some start to hallucinate. I remember one trainee next to me saying he saw sharks swimming up next to him. He freaked out and quit SEAL training right then and there.

In our lifesaving training, none of us were ever told we were good enough at saving lives and permitted to get out of the water. Instead, the instructors in charge would sit in their heated trucks with megaphone speakers on the roof and let us know that if anyone wanted to quit training, they could join the instructors in the warmth and share some hot chocolate. For BUD/S students on the verge of dropping out, it was an alluring option. Chris and I, despite both growing up swimming in the cold waters off New England, were just as miserable as anyone else, but we looked at each other, shivering and shaking, and started to laugh uncontrollably. It was such a ridiculous situation that we couldn't help ourselves. Soon, we had other students around us laughing too. Before long, the instructors were watching an entire class of SEAL trainees laughing about being in the freezing water, laughing through our forced torture.

Chris and I, along with our classmates, learned that no matter how hard something may seem, it is only as hard as you allow it to be. Months later, after graduating from training, one of the instructors I admired most pulled me aside and told me he remembered that day in the water, and that what Chris and I had done demonstrated exactly what the SEALs need: leaders who can look beyond the misery of a situation and help others do the same. Sometimes you have no choice but to look beyond the misery. It's the only way to survive the toughest times.

That isn't the only memory I have of laughing through training—far from it. I remember one time, we were all brought out into the courtyard of the barracks during a "room inspection" and made to bend over and touch our heads to the ground, legs straight, our elbows at a 90-degree angle. It's a physical position that is nearly impossible for any human to hold for more than about 5 seconds—and we were told to stay that way for an hour. Minutes in, my friend Job Price, a tough SEAL and great leader, started to crack up with guttural, full-body laughter. Pretty soon, the entire class was laughing uncontrollably. There's nothing a BUD/S instructor can do—no matter how intimidating he tries to be—to get twenty people to stop laughing at the sheer misery and absurdity of what they're being asked to do.

+ + +

You wouldn't think the SEALs would be a popular place for practical jokes, but over the course of my career, I was involved in so many memorable ones—and it all comes back to strategic control over your emotions. You have to know when it's okay to lighten the mood—indeed, when that's the best possible thing you can do—to energize yourself and your team, build camaraderie, restore focus and commitment, or artfully get someone back in line, if needed.

For instance, one of my habitually late teammates once fell asleep while we were waiting at an airport gate for a no-fail, don't-miss-it trip. I got fifteen SEALs to silently move out of sight, and had the nice lady sitting next to my teammate tap him on the shoulder and awaken him by asking, "Weren't you traveling with that large group that just left?"

In another case, I nearly set off an international diplomatic crisis when we "proved" to our Peruvian counterparts that we Americans had nuclear-tipped bullets by shooting our rifles and simultaneously setting off huge hidden demolition charges in the same direction.

One time, we put a cast on a guy's arm after he'd had a blackout evening of too many drinks, and convinced him that he'd broken it, supporting our story with fake X-rays—and we laughed for over a week as our story became his own story (we had our teammates ask him to recount the tale over and over again that week) to the point where he didn't believe us when we told him his arm wasn't actually broken.

And in Iraq, I drafted a fake letter from Navy headquarters telling my friend that his application for an officer program was received two days late due to slow mail out of the combat zone, but adding that he was "enthusiastically encouraged to apply again next year." (In reality, he was a tremendous candidate for the officer program, and was accepted. He was one of just four SEALs chosen that year—and one of two from my team, the first time two SEALs from the same team were picked. The two of them were each awarded a Bronze Star for combat valor on that deployment, and through the officer program, they attended four years of college and returned to the SEALs as incredible leaders.)

I'm full of stories just like these. There can be well-chosen opportunities for fun even in—or perhaps especially in—the most intense situations.

+ + +

The flipside is that when laughter and fun are not appropriate, you need to be able to rein yourself in. And when there is true danger, you need to be able to stay just as calm and controlled as you would be otherwise. That was my lesson in the Toyota Land Cruiser in Peru. No matter the crisis, it will be worse if you're not calm. My platoon was once training in the Altamaha River in Georgia, and we had an enthusiastic new SEAL named Max. We were carrying kayaks with a good amount of gear inside, trying to find the most convenient way to transport guns, paddles, and sensitive reconnaissance equipment that had to stay dry as we waded through shallow water. Suddenly, Max very calmly stopped and said to me, "Mr. Hayes, there's a gator on my leg."

His calm demeanor in the face of such an alarming statement caused me to doubt him—until he lifted his leg out of the water, and I saw that a 3- or 4-foot baby alligator had indeed latched around his knee. Max, to his extreme credit, did not overreact. He stayed calm—certainly calmer than I would have been—and took deep breaths until the alligator decided to open his mouth and let go. (Max was unharmed—other than his four bite-mark tooth scars.)

Many of our enemies are not as cooperative as that baby alligator ended up being. Which is why our reactions to situations are so important. The smartest SEAL isn't the one with the greatest raw intelligence. It's the one who has the best and quickest reaction to a problem. The SEAL who can quickly assess and decide the best course of action is the one I want on my team, not the SEAL who gets emotional and lets his feelings—or his fears—get in the way of pure rationality. I said in chapter 1 that I would take someone with hunger over someone with greater ability every time. I'd also take someone who reacts well over someone with greater raw intelligence. You want both—intelligence and control—but in the stressful moments, control matters, a lot. I would love to find people who are smart enough to predict the future—but I haven't come across many of them. So I need people who react well, no matter what the future turns out to hold. No matter the context, the importance of having good, controlled reactions to surprising situations can never be overstated.

And honestly, it's easier to train emotional control than raw intelligence. None of us are born great leaders who react perfectly every time. We do the thinking and growing along the way. We put ourselves in the uncomfortable situations to test ourselves and to practice—and over time, we get better and better at maintaining control. We're not designed to be perfect at this. These are our body and brain's automatic responses. But, with work, we can train ourselves to overcome them.

The practical tips will be different for each of us. From the stories I've already told, you can see that laughter is a big part of it for me. If I can find the humor in a situation—even a tense one—it can defuse some of the fear and make me think more clearly. If I can find an ally—a teammate, a buddy, even a friend who isn't in the trenches with me but who I can call on the phone to talk through a problem with—I can move a step closer to realizing that I can handle whatever the current situation calls for.

Keeping the big picture in mind—understanding that the discomfort will pass, that the body and the mind will get used to whatever situation we're in, faster than we realize—can also help me retain my composure. Going outside my body—thinking about what I would tell someone else in the same situation, the advice I would give a teammate or family member—is another trick that works for me and many others.

+ + +

All this leads to a lesson I call "Be a Machine." However you get there, don't let your emotions control you. Do what makes the situation better, not necessarily what makes you feel better. In a crisis, emotion is more often a destructive force than a helpful one. It can motivate us to perform at our best, but it can also distract us from the goal and cause unintended negative consequences. Emotions help us at times, allowing us to act with compassion and warmth, but during difficult situations, we need to put our emotions aside and approach our decisions in a clearsighted, rational way. As a SEAL, I've had to learn just how critical it is to keep my feelings in check when there are bigger issues to consider.

I was halfway through my deployment in Afghanistan, leading SEAL Team TWO and in charge of our operations across a huge swath of the country. The work involved life-or-death decisions every single day, deciding people's fates and figuring out how we were going to reach our strategic goals. The extreme and unbelievable reports from the field rolled in regularly—teenage suicide bombers blowing themselves up in crowds of peaceloving Afghans; massive roadside bombs detonating and vaporizing entire vehicles; Taliban enemies joining the Afghan army in order to launch insider attacks—but on this one particular day, the Taliban had shot six children, killing three, and blamed it on us, as we were conducting operations nearby. There were articles in the media, questions I needed to answer, investigations I was involved with—and protests against us, being incited by the Taliban as part of their strategy to cast us as aggressors.

So I was fighting a real war, a media war, and a war against false propaganda being spread to civilians on the ground.

While this was going on, an immediate family member back home was suffering through a medical crisis that had arisen on the very same day. I couldn't be there, and I felt so conflicted. If I left Afghanistan, I would be putting people's lives at real and immediate risk. And yet at home, I feared things could quickly take a turn for the worse—and, particularly given travel time from the war zone, I felt very far away.

I called my close friend and former White House Fellow classmate Brian, a brilliant, selfless doctor in Boston, and asked for help. (As with all White House Fellows, and any true friend, his answer was "yes" before I even finished my sentence.) I needed Brian to take charge, and he jumped right in. He set up appointments with specialists and oversaw my loved one's medical care. He was more than happy to help, of course—and we'll talk more in chapter 8 about the importance of having people in our lives who we can count on, no matter the circumstance, and being the people others can count on in return—but I still felt torn about where I was and the work I had no choice but to focus on. I don't think I've ever allowed stress to get in my way as a SEAL, but that day felt almost overwhelming. Even now, I still tear up when I think about this situation and Brian's generous and incredible help.

Nevertheless, no matter how much I was struggling personally, I knew I needed to be a rock. For my team, and for the organization, I needed to be the person to pull others up, set the right tone, and keep everyone else on track, even in my hardest time. After the crisis had passed—after the personal situation had stabilized, the investigations had ended, and the immediate war concerns abated a bit—I told my second-in-command, Rocky, who is a world-class SEAL officer and one of my closest friends, what had been going on. He said, "I never would have known."

Now, that's not a perfect lesson. If I was giving advice to someone else in this situation, I would tell them to ask for help. Not like I asked my friend Brian to help manage the medical issue, but to help in person on the battlefield, because we shouldn't have to bear these burdens alone. I did ask Rocky to keep an eye on me, just in case things got too overwhelming, but I probably asked too late, and there was probably more help I could have asked for earlier on. I'll talk later in this book about how asking for help is a strength, not a weakness—but it's also the case that you can't let yourself fall apart when your team needs you. When you're in a situation where you are responsible for things more important than your own personal circumstances, you have to remain in control for the good of everyone around you. You have to be a machine. Had things become unmanageable, I would have of course asked for whatever help I needed, but given the combat circumstances and significant daily risks, the thing I knew I needed to do was remain in control and put my Task Force ahead of my own needs.

+ + +

The hardest part, no question, is when the work has to compete with family and with those you love. Those situations become the most uncomfortable, and the most difficult to manage. By 2012, as a country, we were close to our tenth year in Afghanistan. When a war starts, there's zero infrastructure. You eat, drink, and wear what you bring into battle or what gets airdropped to you. After a few months, the chow hall might be a tent, and there might be a makeshift store selling soap, toothpaste, and the barest provisions. By year ten, there are chain restaurants, ice cream shops, and local vendors selling anything they can. Headquarters grows to become an established base, a fully functional settlement within a country. My base in Afghanistan—housing just special ops, much more remote than the larger facilities, no brand-name ice cream—was more like a city that hadn't yet been built. We turned our lights out at night so the Taliban wouldn't be able to aim their indirect weapons—mortars and rockets— right at us. Still, we were rocketed something like twenty-eight out of thirty nights at one point, the enemy taking lucky shots at us, which at times came far too close. We had an audible warning system in place to tell us when rockets were incoming so we could find cover as quickly as possible.

You live with this long enough and it becomes routine, even though when you take a step back, nothing about it sounds routine at all. I had Skype in my room, so, unlike many in a combat zone, I was able to talk to my wife and daughter with some frequency. My room was at the end of a building, in a back corner. One evening, I was on Skype and suddenly there was a loud explosion in our compound, right outside my bedroom wall. A rocket landed not 20 meters from my room, sending debris flying off my ceiling and walls. The explosive bass resonated deeply in my chest cavity. Luckily, there was a concrete wall between me and the explosion, but I couldn't help but flinch, and my family, of course, couldn't help but hear that something had happened.

"That was a close one," I said out loud without thinking. I had intentionally been keeping my family in the dark about our frequent rocket attacks—they didn't need to know, and I didn't want them to worry. But now they had heard one—and for their benefit, I needed to make it seem like this was routine, normal, and unexceptional. "It's no big deal," I said. "We're just getting rocketed again." I couldn't have chosen worse words.

The explosion had obviously scared them, but I knew I needed to hang up quickly and go make sure everything (and everyone) was okay. There was no way to quickly get off the phone and keep them from worrying about me, but my job, in that moment, was to stay calm, not just for myself and my team, but also for my family, to manage their emotions and be the best husband and father I could be, even from so far away. I had trained myself to be a machine, to remain cool and calm even in a life-or-death situation.

Of course, when I got back to the States, I told them how disappointed I was that I had added to their stress that day, and for the rest of that deployment. Anyone in a combat zone has no choice but to deal with the constant risk—the chance, as we drive down roads rigged to explode, or merely sit in our rooms, Skyping with our families, that any given moment will be our last. I did sometimes wonder as I went to sleep if I would wake up the next morning. Three times we thwarted very real attempts by a VBIED (vehicle-borne improvised explosive device, or, in plain English, a truck that brought us our gas looking to drive in and blow itself up on our compound). I had actually placed my bed as far away from the exterior wall as possible, as if being an extra four feet from an explosion would save me. But despite these real and unavoidable risks, we do have the choice and usually the ability to try to shield our loved ones from as much of that emotional turmoil as we can. I'll always wish I could have handled that one a little differently.

+ + +

I tell this story to illustrate the struggle. We can't—and shouldn't—erase emotion from our lives. We can't be good partners, friends, spouses, and parents without emotion, without feelings, without vulnerability and genuine honesty. But we also can't be effective performers if we aren't able to compartmentalize, to put those feelings aside when they're not helpful to the situation at hand. We need to be able to react well to whatever circumstance presents itself, and we need to remember that calm breeds calm.

It's only with emotional control, by being our best even when things are at their worst, that we can most effectively help and serve the people around us. In the next chapter, armed with a hunger to learn and grow, and the strength and control to remain calm in any situation, we'll turn to what we can do with these skills—namely, focus on others and make sure we orient ourselves toward truthfulness, integrity, and aid to the people around us.

We must act with accountability, humility, and scrupulous honesty to set our egos aside, and understand how to employ our gifts and talents, but at the same time recognize that we can never know everything. Living with both humility and confidence is the last of the three lessons that make us truly excellent in whatever situation we encounter.

CHAPTER 3

LIVE WITH INCREDIBLE CONFIDENCE AND EXTREME HUMILITY

Excellence in Accountability and Orientation

A decade into my SEAL career, I went to the Harvard Kennedy School for two years to earn a master's degree. After, I went back to command SEAL Team TEN in Iraq, and then, three years later, when I was thirty-seven years old, I was privileged to serve as a White House Fellow under Presidents George W. Bush and Barack Obama. President Lyndon Johnson started the White House Fellows program in 1964 to provide government and leadership experience to young professionals across the country, from a range of careers. President Johnson hoped that exposing young leaders to a firsthand view of how government works from the inside would inspire these professionals to find ways to contribute to the nation when the fellowship was over.

The program was and is highly competitive, with thousands applying each year, winnowed down by a series of essays that applicants write about their lives, their influences, the kinds of people they are, and the impact they want to have on the world. I was chosen as one of one hundred regional finalists, then one of thirty-two national finalists, at which point each of us was interviewed by thirty-two nationally known judges over three days in an intense round-the-clock marathon to choose a class of fourteen fellows. No two fellows are posed the same questions. I was asked about the biggest ethical dilemma I'd ever faced and failed. I was asked what I would say to the President if we had 45 seconds together in an elevator. I was asked about the influence my mother had on my life. I was asked what one national policy I would change if I had the power, and how I would change it. The answers were important, of course, but the judges also wanted to see evidence of how I thought, how I communicated, and whether I was able to maintain poise, gravitas, and amiability.

I talked in the previous chapter about being comfortable with discomfort—trust me, this was an intense set of conversations where it would have been easy to lose my composure. Now, as an interviewer, on the other side of the process, I know they weren't just looking for smart people with impressive résumés. They want people who have the potential to change the world.

What was most special about the program was that we got real jobs in the administration, critical roles of genuine responsibility, working with cabinet secretaries, senior staff, or top White House officials. After selection, each fellow's résumé is passed to leaders throughout the executive branch. We were interviewed and ultimately offered a position—or a choice of them. One of my interviews was with an incredibly impressive man with a long history of distinguished service to the nation, who was then one of President Bush's senior-most officials. He was interviewing three people—two lifelong DC policy experts and me—to find someone to help lead our nation's defense policy and strategy, overseeing the various departments and agencies in the executive branch. The job included figuring out which issues to pay most attention to, advancing the policies or actions the nation needed most, running meetings, navigating the politics between stakeholders, and, at that particular moment in time, working to hammer out a new deal for a Russian nuclear treaty, a situation where a whole bunch of different people were having trouble coming to an agreement. My interviewer sat me down and asked a bunch of introductory questions, then stared at me with intensity and said, "Mike, what do you know about the START treaty?"

I took a breath, looked at him, and said, with deadpan seriousness, "I know how to spell it." Honestly, I didn't know anything about our nation's nuclear treaties, not a bit. But what I did know—and I told him this, too—was how to get the right people into a room and how to run a decision-making process. I knew how to figure out what motivated people, how to get them to generate ideas, how to cooperate, and, ultimately, how to leave the room with the best possible outcome.

I wasn't afraid to admit that I didn't know a thing about nuclear policy—and I think that was what got me the job. Being humble enough to admit what you don't know but still confident enough to explain where you can add value is a balance that is often hard to strike. But you need to recognize that it's a strength, not a weakness, to know what's beyond your knowledge or understanding at any point in time, instead of pretending otherwise.

I walk into any room and always assume the people in it are smarter than I am, faster than I am, and more agile than I am. That way, I can never be wrong. I never assume I have *the* idea. I have *an* idea. Maybe it's the best one, or maybe it's not, but honestly, it shouldn't even matter, because our job in any room is to find the best answer for the problem we're working on, no matter whose answer it is. We have to listen to each other, and really hear each other—and the best way to do that is to walk into the room knowing that there's no doubt that everyone in there has something useful to say.

Not more than three weeks after that interview, I was in the White House Situation Room with experts who knew everything that I didn't, but who couldn't get on the same page about it and had been unable to agree on proposed draft language for the nuclear treaty. I got them all in the room for our very first meeting and shut the door. "I've been a Navy SEAL for fifteen years," I told them. "You know a lot more about nuclear policy than I do, but I'm great at keeping a door closed and not letting anyone out of here until we see some compromise and work things out."

They laughed, but I was serious. I had already figured out that people in Washington like to play power games with each other, pretending they can't agree to something unless their boss approves, thinking the idea of it being escalated up the chain will scare people into submission. I needed to prevent anyone from being able to pull that maneuver, from stalling progress in order to get their way. I said, "There's a hundred-fifty-plus years of DC experience in this room, and yet you still can't figure this out? Who in here thinks your boss is smarter than you on these issues? Who thinks your boss knows more of the details and should be in here instead?" Of course, no one raised a hand. "Great. So we have the smartest people in Washington on this subject in this room right now. Let's get it done."

I wanted the people in the room to see the bigger picture. I talked about what it meant to me to be in that room and what I felt as an American serving my country. I hoped to appeal to the same motivations they had, and remind them why they had chosen to work in government. There were five months left in the Bush administration at that point, and I knew they didn't want to leave this for the next President. I just had to harness that motivation in the service of actually finding agreement.

A few weeks later, I was part of our fifteen-person interagency delegation, and one of two people from the White House, to go to Moscow to negotiate START (the Strategic Arms Reduction Treaty) with the Russians. Once again, I knew what I knew, and I knew what I didn't know. I knew a lot more about START by then, but the others in the delegation were the domain experts. Some had spent their careers working to understand the delicate politics of the region, and others had decades of experience dealing with the substance of the nuclear armament issue. I was simply the guy who had brought us to consensus. I needed to be humble enough to let others take the lead when their skills were the ones we most needed in the moment, and confident enough that I didn't need to prove my worth and ultimately hurt the mission by trying to do what might be better handled by someone else.

You can train yourself to do the hard things, and you can practice being comfortable in the most trying situations, but you're not going to be the most effective performer unless you have the right attitude about the people around you. You have to understand your own gifts and talents, absolutely, and bring them forward when useful—but at the same time, you also have to recognize that we can never know everything. We all have to orient ourselves to rely on others, set our egos aside, and ask for help when we need it. We have to be honest and accountable, and live with integrity and transparency. True excellence means accepting blame even more quickly than we take credit, and sharing that credit with everyone around us. Without that attitude, we simply aren't excellent enough.

+ + +

I tell that story about START to illustrate the point that being humble and being confident aren't in conflict. Lots of people think the two ideas are opposites, but they're not. Being humble doesn't mean having a lack of confidence. All we have on every topic is varied levels of ignorance. None of us is going to be the best in the room at everything. No one has it all figured out. That's the humility piece of it. And perhaps ironically, it takes confidence to be appropriately humble, to be able to admit that others may be smarter, faster, and stronger, and to be willing to reverse course if the situation calls for it.

Confidence and humility are not different points on the same line. They are entirely different axes and states of mind. You can be confident that you have something to contribute, and at the same time recognize that you're not the only one who has value to add. It takes confidence to give credit to others, to let your teammates shine, to give more than you take, to admit when you've made a mistake, to change a plan, and to be fully honest and transparent about everything you are doing. I grew up with the understanding that we must succeed at all costs—and the

SEALs largely believed in that ethos when I was first starting out. But after just a few years of combat in a world at war, we realized as a special operations force—and I realized as a human being—that success means you pull back when it makes sense to pull back, and you reverse course if that's what will lead to greater victory going forward. As I've said before, you don't assume risk that isn't worth assuming. This kind of thinking requires humility—to admit, freely, that you may have been wrong when planning the mission—and the utmost confidence to trust your instincts even when it means adjusting on the fly.

This kind of no-holds-barred security in your own standing lets you put the organization above yourself, and do the right thing even when the right thing is hard (chapter 1), uncomfortable (chapter 2), or may carry consequences—physical, interpersonal, or hierarchical, just to name three examples—that you'd rather not face. From my career, I've drawn three lessons that circle around these issues, and that together explain the kind of orientation the most successful and high-impact people approach the world with: community comes first; live with integrity and transparency; and assume everything you do will end up on the front page of the newspaper (because, as you'll see at the end of this chapter, sometimes that's exactly what happens).

Let's look at each of these lessons individually.

Community Comes First

I hate to say it, but this one's easy. Back in SEAL training, we were out in the water doing boat drills. Two of our boats were right next to each other, so close to getting past that last wave and beyond the surf zone. But that final wave was huge—and it flipped both boats at the same time. As we were all being thrown into the water, on the boat next to mine, one guy's paddle hit another SEAL trainee in the face, hard. He was floating upside down, bleeding profusely and not moving. I saw it happen, and as the person closest to him, instinct took over, just as it would for any student in the class. I swam to him, grabbed him, and dragged him ashore. We became lifelong friends, and of course I never missed an opportunity to jokingly remind him how I saved his life. Truth is, I was just the guy nearest to the situation. What I did wasn't hard—it was necessary, and it was natural, given the circumstances. Any of us would have done the exact same thing—and I'm certain of that, because you can't get through training without absorbing this lesson: team, then teammate, then self.

It's the SEAL hierarchy, and it becomes yours over time, almost part of your DNA. You think of others before you consider yourself. You focus on giving more than taking. You give up opportunities and hand them off to others so that they can grow. It was the same lesson I learned in college as part of the Jesuit ethos at Holy Cross: others before self. It's easy to do things for yourself, because it's easy to know what will satisfy you the most—but it's far harder to do things in a way that keeps others at the forefront of your mind.

When I was a very young officer, just out of training myself, I had a SEAL on my team who was older and more experienced than I was—I'll call him Stan. Despite Stan's age and years of service, as an enlisted SEAL (not an officer), I was his "officer in charge," as the SEALs refer to it. One day, Stan and I were riding in a car together in Santiago, Chile. We were stopped at a red light, watching an elderly woman slowly cross the street.

Our light turned green, and the woman was still in the intersection. Stan had been eating Wheat Thins, and suddenly, he yelled at the woman to hurry up and began to throw his crackers at her. This was wrong on so many levels. As soon as my brain registered what was happening, I cut Stan off and stopped the behavior, instantly. I calmly but forcefully said, "Stan, put your window up right now, and don't say another word until we are back at our hotel." I was furious, embarrassed, and deeply sorry that a SEAL, or any human being, would act that way.

There were so many things going through my mind over the rest of that ride. I couldn't believe Stan would disrespect another person like that. And I couldn't believe that he would risk the reputation of the SEALs and of our country in the process. I wanted to scream at him. I wanted to yell, tell him all the ways in which his behavior was a disgrace, embarrass him, humiliate him. That would have felt good to me. But it wouldn't have changed the way he acted going forward. It wouldn't have helped him become a better SEAL, or a better person.

So I thought about it. I stayed calm on that ride back to the hotel and tried to collect my thoughts. I knew that the most important thing was to react logically instead of emotionally. Just as we talked about in the last chapter, emotional control is critical. Once the wave of anger had passed, I thought about how Stan had told me that he wanted to work on his writing, and that he wanted to become a better communicator. So I tailored his consequences toward that goal. I told him he owed me a three-page essay about what he did. I said that if he felt like he would do the same thing again, he could argue why it was appropriate; otherwise, he could explain why it was wrong, and what he had learned. I knew he wouldn't choose the first option, but I wanted the analysis to come from within himself, not just from me yelling at him.

He came back to me with an essay that hit several of the points I would have made, and we talked through the others that he didn't pick up on. We talked about how he could handle himself better in the future. He learned what he had done wrong—but, on a subconscious level, he also learned how to effectively influence and discipline others. In the end, he thanked me for the punishment—and years later, he thanked me again. He thanked me for knowing him well enough to give him a meaningful punishment, and caring enough to think about what would best serve him, instead of just venting my own anger at him and making it all about me. It's a small story, but I think it illustrates how to apply the idea of "others before self" even in situations that don't seem like they matter. Because they do matter. Every moment matters. In everything you do, you can think about how to best serve the people around you, and how to best serve the community.

A decision to discipline someone isn't about making yourself, as the leader, feel better—it's about making people understand where they fell short, helping them to change their actions in the future, and altering their perspective. And then, ultimately, it's about serving the organization better. Every SEAL with us in Santiago knew about Stan's punishment—and every SEAL who would go on to become a leader in the organization saw an example of meaningful discipline. Stan went on to have a long career as a SEAL—and not only am I pretty sure he never again disrespected a local crossing the street, he also helped the junior SEALs he disciplined over the course of his service to become better themselves.

Live with Integrity and Transparency

There is, inevitably, the occasional SEAL who makes it through training but just doesn't fit. Early in my career, I ended up with one of those SEALs on my team: Hal, who was much older than me and had been a SEAL far longer. He was constantly cutting corners, and everyone knew it. After a series of poor performances, he ended up ostracized by my entire platoon. He didn't belong, and he needed to either improve or leave. I decided I had to take action for the good of the team, so I called him into my office and laid out the entire case that had been built against him, the behaviors we had noticed, and the situations where he hadn't lived up to his obligations as a SEAL. I asked him if he thought he had done well enough, but he refused to engage, and refused to admit there was anything he could be doing better.

I told Hal that I had no choice but to write him up for poor performance—which, in the SEALs, is a big deal. My report would be placed in his record, would be part of his annual performance evaluation, and could potentially be used down the road to remove him from the SEALs and send him home. I remember with certainty that this was the first time I had ever said, "I'll have to write you up." It wasn't typical, and it was especially unusual because I was a young officer dealing with someone who had been a SEAL for much longer.

When someone is written up, part of the process is that they are required to sign the report, to show that the person making the report has discussed it with them. And Hal blew me away when he told me he wouldn't sign the report.

I had no witnesses in the room with me, which turned out to be a mistake, because what Hal said next truly shocked me. He told me that if I made him sign the report, and wouldn't throw it away like it had never existed, he would make up lies about me with the intention of ruining my career. The easiest thing to do in that moment would have been to ratchet down the situation, try to backtrack and explain to Hal that maybe we could work this out, consider this a warning, not make him sign the report, then use back channels to get him transferred or moved so he'd become someone else's problem.

But I wasn't going to let someone threaten me like that—and I wasn't going to let someone who would do such a thing remain a SEAL, not if I could help it. It was clear from his actions that the behaviors in the report were only the tip of the iceberg, and that he was not someone we could have on the battlefield. Any risk to my own career—or at least the prospect of being dragged into a battle over who said what—had to be secondary. Without hesitating, I made him sign the report.

Hal was out of the Navy by the next year, after a year-end evaluation ended up stalling his career. The experience did teach me a lesson, though: in situations that have the potential to turn hostile, always have a witness.

+ + +

A somewhat similar situation took place when I was a young officer, and it's worth examining to make a different point. We were down in Florida on a dive training trip. Bill, a senior chief (the second-highest enlisted rank) in his mid-thirties, had come along as one of the trainers working with a new group of SEALs; he was not at all thrilled that I, still in my early twenties, was the highest-ranking person on the trip. One night, several of us ended up at a hot dog stand at around three in the morning.

Bill, hot-tempered and maybe just a little bit drunk, got into an unnecessary verbal altercation with the vendor, then picked up a bottle of mustard from the stand and squirted it all over the man. I saw this and knew I had to do something. It wasn't like this was a matter of national security, but SEALs cannot risk earning a bad reputation in the local community. There is no such thing as an "off-duty" SEAL. Our fellow citizens expect and deserve the best from us, every hour of the day. What hurts the organization hurts the country—and in any case, grown adults shouldn't behave like Bill had.

When I ordered him back to the hotel, Bill protested—but I pulled rank, one of the rare times I ever said, "This is a direct order." I told him that if something like this happened again, I would get my boss, the senior officer back at my team's headquarters in Virginia Beach, to bring him home from the trip for improper behavior. Make no mistake, being sent back from a training trip carries real consequences, and not just for the person being sent home. It costs the entire team training time and makes us weaker. It's not something to be taken lightly. The very next night, I heard from other members of the team that Bill had gone back to the hot dog stand and had again caused trouble. I called a senior officer back in Virginia Beach and explained the situation, then outlined my plan. He could have taken over from there, removed the matter from my hands and dealt with Bill himself. But even though Bill was more than a decade my senior, this was my team, and my responsibility. I wasn't going to simply pass the buck on this, report Bill, and then throw up my hands and claim to be uninvolved in the consequences of my decision. When I got off the phone, I went to Bill directly, and I sent him home.

Part of living with integrity and transparency is owning what you do, and being able to stand up and defend every action you take. I talk sometimes about the idea of stabbing people in the heart, not the back (figuratively, of course!). We hash things out face-to-face, as individuals, not through back-channel communications—just like in that White House Situation Room meeting I wrote about earlier, where I insisted that everyone lay their cards on the table while we were all in the room, not through emails and anonymous gossip after the fact. If you won't say something to someone's face, maybe you shouldn't be saying it at all. And if you can't defend your actions to the people those actions will affect the most, then maybe you ought to rethink the legitimacy of what you're doing. People can learn to become better—just like I knew Stan could—but sometimes, when you see true issues with someone's character and values, like I had with Bill and Hal, you need to take action and confront them.

+ + +

At the Harvard Kennedy School, where I studied for two years on a scholarship from the Navy before becoming a White House Fellow, I encountered a situation that paralleled these. While I was sitting in class one day, a professor announced that he suspected a particular student had been cheating—and I knew, with complete certainty, that the professor was wrong. I had worked with that classmate, who had become an instant friend, and I knew he had completed the assignment in question by himself. There were eighty people in the room, and we were just a few weeks into the semester. No one wants to speak up in a moment like that, contradict a professor, and risk their own standing. But what kind of person would I be if I let it go, told myself it wasn't my problem, and allowed things to play out on their own? What kind of behavior would I be enabling with my silence?

I stood up, and I spoke up. I told the professor that what he was doing wasn't okay, that he was making a false accusation, and that he couldn't be more wrong. I held my ground and the professor backed down, softened his tone, and pivoted the comments into some general (and unnecessary) "don't cheat" remarks addressed to the whole class. My friend was grateful that I spoke up, but earning his gratitude wasn't why I did it. I had to be able to look in the mirror and know that I was on the side of truth and integrity. If you're not standing up for what's right, how can you expect anyone else to?

Assume Everything You Do Will End Up on the Front Page of the Newspaper

"The three Navy SEALs stomped on the bound Afghan detainees and dropped heavy stones on their chests, the witnesses recalled. They stood on the prisoners' heads and poured bottles of water on some of their faces in what, to a pair of Army soldiers, appeared to be an improvised form of waterboarding."

—"Navy SEALs, a Beating Death and Claims of a Cover-Up," by Nicholas Kulish, Christopher Drew, and Matthew Rosenberg, *New York Times*, December 17, 2015

It was not a great morning to be a SEAL, I have to be honest. When I saw the headline in the *New York Times*, I knew the article was going to be a difficult read. It was about a situation that took place in Kalach, Afghanistan, a mountainous village in the southern part of the country, back in 2012. A bomb exploded at a checkpoint where my SEAL Team was grooming a local police unit of peace-loving Afghans to fight for their own country. These were people taking a risk for a better future, to try to help advance their own principles of life and liberty. One of those Afghan police officers died in the explosion, and the rest of his team was furious. They knew the locals and could identify the transient Taliban members in town. These Afghan police officers found and captured the guys who they believed had killed their friend.

And then things went very poorly.

On their way to the American base, these Afghan police allegedly beat the captured Taliban fighters "with rifle butts and car antennas," according to the *Times'* account. And when they arrived at their destination, three SEALs from my team were said to have joined in. One of the Taliban men reportedly died later that day, supposedly from the abuse he suffered at the hands of the Afghan police and, allegedly, the three SEALs.

I was not on hand when these events were taking place. As the Commander of SEAL Team TWO and our Special Operations Task Force in southeastern Afghanistan (SOTF-SE) at the time, I was in charge of roughly two thousand individuals—around two hundred SEALs and eighteen hundred other military personnel—across approximately two dozen stations in the region. Each station was a little different, but there were always three lines of operation: security (tasked with strike operations against the Taliban), governance (responsible for helping the Afghans establish local governments and take over the running of their country from our military forces), and civil (in charge of helping to build infrastructure, repair roads, and make the region more habitable for the locals).

As soon as the story of what had happened in Kalach made it back to me, I was immediately concerned. Under the Geneva Convention, once they are taken captive, detainees like these Taliban fighters must be treated as our own men. They can never be abused, and it is a gross mishandling of a human life for something like this to happen. At the point when I heard the allegations, they were unproven, but I very quickly did some due diligence and found there was enough probability of wrongdoing—though I couldn't be certain of the specifics—that immediate action needed to be taken. An organization can never effectively investigate itself, so I called the Naval Criminal Investigative Service (NCIS) and had them flown in as quickly as possible from the large multinational military base in Kandahar.

I should note that just because the word "Naval" is in their name doesn't mean NCIS was bound to find that our guys did nothing wrong. NCIS is an absolutely professional organization of unbiased investigators whose only job is to get to the truth. Truth always makes organizations stronger. After their investigation, I felt confident that we would be able to say with credibility and confidence that the allegations were true, or that they weren't—and if they were true, we would be able to get to the root cause of the situation and identify where we could improve.

I isolated the accused SEALs, flew them to my headquarters, and had their guns taken away. I sent them home, fired them from the deployment, and recommended that they be kicked out of the SEALs.

This was hard for me, because I knew these men, and I believed them to be highly capable and good human beings who had made a grievous error. I want to believe that in most cases, people can be trained to become better, to fix their flaws, and to learn how to operate at a higher level in everything they do—that's fundamentally why I was driven to write this book and share my stories. But I believed those men had acted in ways that clearly crossed the line and had shown flaws in character and judgment that meant they did not belong on the SEAL Teams.

After sending the men home, I had no contact with them—the disciplinary and legal process made it unwise to speak with them along the way. In the end, despite my recommendation that the men be kicked out of the Navy, I was overruled by my boss, a SEAL who was administratively in charge of all the SEAL Teams on the East Coast. He did not fire them from the SEALs, and that's why, three years later, the article written in the *Times* was framed as if there had been a cover-up. Witnesses were influenced to change their stories, according to the *Times* report, and ultimately, the charges against the SEALs were dismissed.

That changed after the article appeared. The case was re-opened due to public pressure, and for more than two years, the accused SEALs were again involved in legal proceedings over the incident. Then, in late 2019, the charges were once again dropped, with the military prosecutors explaining that the now seven-year-old evidence had degraded and convictions were unlikely—but that's not the point here. The point is that I woke up that morning in December 2015, and in the potentially terrifying time between seeing the headline and reading the story, I wasn't worried about what the article was going to say about me personally. I knew I had acted with integrity. I had taken their weapons right away, gone to the investigators, and made the case for their discharge from service. I knew there was nothing more that I could have done, and that I had nothing to be ashamed of.

It's not that I was certain that the SEALs were guilty as charged. My due diligence and my letter recommending termination were just two inputs into the overall process. I could have accepted the decision to drop the charges if I thought that decision had emerged from a good and thorough process. I wasn't trying to predetermine right and wrong. My responsibility—everyone's responsibility—was to gather and provide honest information. We can stand up for what we believe in and still trust and follow a sensible process. Indeed, we need good processes in order to reach the best conclusions (I'll talk much more about decision-making processes in chapter 5).

In fact, after the decision was ultimately made to keep the men in the SEALs, I pulled them into my office for a talk. I told them that I had advocated for kicking them out, but clearly that hadn't happened. I told them I accepted the decision to return them to the team, supported the process, and wanted them to understand that the goal now was to learn from the situation and become better SEALs—and human beings—going forward. I encouraged them to reflect and improve, and emphasized how deeply I wanted them to succeed as SEALs and in life. While I know they surely didn't appreciate that I had taken the position that they should have been kicked out, I also know they respected that I was telling them to their faces, and then encouraging them to be the best SEALs and people they could be. The reality of the process was that I had done everything I could to make my case for the outcome I thought was right, but now I had to work with them, and I was going to try to make our work together as productive as it could possibly be.

+ + +

Not everything we do will end up being on the front page of the newspaper, but we have to act as if someone is always watching. We should never wake up wondering if today is the day our true nature will be revealed. Our true nature should be something we are proud to present to the world and can stand behind with honor.

In the end, after the *Times* article was published and the case subsequently reopened, I was contacted by the Navy's lawyers as a witness. It pulled me back into the events of years before. At one point along the way, I sent an email to one of the accused men. I knew he wouldn't respond to it, but I wanted him to know that all was not necessarily lost for his future. I reminded him that despite the circumstances, and despite the serious and regrettable mistakes I believed he had made, I would still be in his corner after all this played out, and I was willing to help him reshape his life and get beyond this terrible event.

Few people are irredeemable. For the years he has left on this planet, why shouldn't the planet get the very best from him that we can? I can never defend the actions he was accused of, but from the two years we had together before those events, I felt with absolute certainty that he had the potential to live the rest of his life as a good man. I knew that if he could make amends—if any of us can ever make amends for the harms we have done in life—why shouldn't we try to salvage what we could, pull each other up, and help each other use the skills and experiences we have to pull up others around us? There are SEALs who could learn from this experience and do better because of that lesson. We can all do better, armed with the examples of people who have improved themselves and taken responsibility for the times they have failed.

+ + +

These first three chapters combine to create what I consider a road map to excellence. Do the hard things, get comfortable with discomfort, orient yourself in the service of others, and live a life of honesty and integrity. Living this way, you set yourself up to be a valuable contributor no matter what situation you find yourself in, and no matter what organization or cause you choose to serve. You become a person who others rely on. You make yourself trusted in any situation.

In the next section of the book, we move from the individual to the team. Once you have committed to your own excellence, how do you apply that excellence to the organizational structure around you? How do you find your role, how do you make decisions, and how do you lead and inspire others? These are the subjects of the next three chapters, and together they form a discussion of agility. We need to be as quick, as flexible, and as decisive as possible in order to maximize our impact and the impact of the teams we serve and lead. Excellence without agility keeps you siloed in pursuit of goals that may well be shifting under your feet. We need to move as targets move, and, like every good SEAL knows, we need to plan, and then also plan for the plan to change. Just like we can never be excellent enough, we can never be dexterous, fleet, or nimble enough as we pursue our highest aspirations.

SECTION II

NEVER AGILE ENOUGH

CHAPTER 4

BE A LEADER AND A FOLLOWER, AND KNOW WHEN TO BE WHICH

Agility in the Roles You Play

Back in 2007, I was second-in-command of SEAL Team TEN and the military's Special Operations Task Force in Anbar Province, Iraq. My team had arrived at the peak of the insurgency: militant Sunni extremists were terrorizing our coalition forces and the peace-wanting citizens of Iraq with regularity, launching attack after attack. In our first month, thirty-five Marines were killed in and around Fallujah alone.

Our job was to embark on nightly missions to capture and eliminate this network of insurgent forces. We would spend each day planning operations and using intelligence to identify terrorist networks, and then each night, we would take helicopters or ground vehicles to pursue our identified targets. We patrolled silently on foot in total darkness, hit our target buildings with controlled and precise violence, separated probable combatants from noncombatants, and decided who to take prisoner for further interrogation in an effort to unravel the insurgency.

We always tried to make it home before sunrise, mostly because it was safer for us to work in the dark, but also because we needed to get as much sleep as possible before waking by noon to repeat the cycle again. This was our life, night after night after night. Our excellent support personnel handled intelligence, dealt with the people we captured, fixed our broken radios and vehicles, and maintained our base camp, letting us focus entirely on the missions themselves.

We saw tremendous success, but it wasn't without cost. On one mission, our forces were headed toward a target building when they passed an Iraqi family—a husband and wife with their two children, eight and ten years old. The parents had lived in the target building, and they confirmed for us that they had been kicked out of their house by violent Sunni extremists, who now occupied the building. As our forces approached, the terrorists opened fire and threw grenades out of the windows directly at the team and the Iraqi family. Lieutenant Jason Redman (who has written his own moving book about his experiences as a SEAL, *The Trident*, as well as a follow-up, *Overcome*) and many others on the team bravely exposed themselves to enemy fire in order to save the family and guide them to protective cover. By moving these innocent Iraqis out of the way, the platoon was able to call in an airstrike, which leveled the building and eliminated all the terrorists inside. These men stepped up and took the ultimate risk for their team and for their country, guiding four innocent people to safety instead of sprinting directly toward cover for themselves.

A few weeks later, our Task Force was in the central Iraqi city of Karma. Karma was known to be filled with insurgents, and it was a risky mission. On the team's way in, they walked through a field of tall, green vegetation. Hidden in this vegetation were four or five insurgents with machine guns who were ready to become martyrs. It's not easy to fight an enemy who is so willing to die. When the insurgents opened fire, Jason immediately went down with multiple shots through his head, arm, and leg. Jason's teammate Luke saw one of the insurgents just a few meters in front of him and went down with a round through his leg that shattered his tibia and fibula just below his knee. In the complete darkness and chaos of combat, the SEALs at the back of the formation were unable to shoot at the enemy, because they couldn't be sure they wouldn't hit their teammates. While those SEALs flanked the enemy, Mitch, the SEAL closest to Luke, had to make a split-second decision.

As the only one who could possibly save Luke, should he move forward, putting himself at mortal risk? Or should he run for cover? It wasn't a decision. It was instinct. Mitch moved forward in a hail of heavy gunfire coming from two directions in order to save Luke. He was hit in the right arm as he moved forward, disintegrating a few inches of bone. He used his other arm to tuck the injured arm into his belt in order to avoid losing it completely and continued forward toward Luke. Mitch then got hit in the leg, but had Luke in his grasp and used a superhero-size reserve of strength and determination to drag him to safety. As Jason fought to stay conscious, and with Mitch and Luke seriously injured, others had to step up.

Jay, our ever-calm SEAL radioman, called in an AC-130 aircraft as he crawled (at his own great risk) to see exactly where the insurgents were and where his teammates had found cover. Jay

gave the pilots explicit instructions about where to aim the grenades from their position more than 10,000 feet in the sky. He
masterfully guided them directly to the enemy positions. And
while Jay knew he was within the potential blast radius, he also
knew that in order to save the rest of his team, he needed the
pilots to release the weapons immediately.

The pilots told Jay that he was "danger close," which meant
he was within the potential blast radius. The pilots required Jay
to acknowledge this, and they also requested something that we
usually only see in SEAL textbooks: they asked him to confirm
his initials as a way of making sure with absolute clarity that he
realized the gravity of the situation and what was about to happen, and to be certain it wasn't an enemy pretending to be him.
They wanted to be sure that he understood the risk.

The pilots, who had been engaged in these kinds of missions night after night, did an incredible job neutralizing the
insurgents, enabling our forces to call in a medical helicopter to
get the wounded to the battlefield hospital in Baghdad. Jason,
Mitch, Luke, Jay, several pilots, and everyone on the mission that
night were heroes, stepping up to save each other and remove
dangerous terrorists from the battlefield.

✦ ✦ ✦

I'm often asked why people make the kinds of sacrifices I just
described. Why would Jason and his team save the Iraqi family? Why would Mitch move forward into such heavy, life-
threatening gunfire? Why would Jay step up and take on so
much risk by authorizing the release of weapons "danger close"?
The "why" is an important question, and the answer draws on
elements that we've covered in earlier chapters, like moving to-

ward the hardest challenges and being oriented toward others over yourself, as well as elements we've yet to cover, like the thoughts ahead about relationships and service to the world. But it's not the only question to ask, and it's not the question I want to address here.

The question for now is a more tactical one: *How* do people do this? How do you know when to step up and when to fall back, when to rush forward into the heavy gunfire (or the less-deadly but still equally important equivalents in your life) and when to let the battle belong to someone else?

When I talk about being the leader of a SEAL Team, people imagine me at the front of every mission, the first one into the building, the one barking orders at everyone behind me. That's just not true—and that's a big part of what makes the SEALs so effective at what we do. There's a line said facetiously but with real merit during Army jump school—where you first learn how to parachute from an aircraft: "YOU are the parachute commander." In that situation, you have to be; it's just you and the parachute. In every other situation, who is leading the charge depends entirely on who is best equipped to do so in that moment, regardless of role and regardless of rank. A moment later, it might be someone else entirely.

As I say in the title of this chapter, you have to see yourself as a leader *and* as a follower, and critically, you have to know when to be which. It's an idea I call "dynamic subordination." In an effective team, we all must seamlessly move forward and back depending on the demands of the situation and the skills of the people around us. We don't get locked into a particular job, a particular task, or a particular pattern: we maintain the agility to be whatever we need to be under the circumstances. Perhaps even more important, we train just as hard to learn how to *be* lots of things as we train to know *when* to be each of those things.

It applies in every sphere. Sometimes you're the leader. Sometimes you're the follower. Sometimes, in the span of just a minute or two, you're both. High-performing teams—and not just in the military—succeed and fail together, with the best players understanding at all moments what will make the mission more successful and what role they need to play to best enable that success.

As we talk about this idea of dynamic subordination, there are four principles it's important to touch on, and I'll cover each one in the rest of this chapter.

The More I Hurt, the Less My Teammates Hurt

Jason Redman and his team obviously understood this point, and it's a fairly clear one on the battlefield. But what sometimes gets overlooked is how much it applies in our everyday lives, no matter what we do. Taking on problems so that others don't have to, doing the hard work, bearing burdens on behalf of your organization—these are the things that make you the kind of person everyone wants to work with. When my daughter was in seventh grade, I spoke to her class about leadership. I told them to think about an assignment where they'd been paired with a partner. When there are two of you working on a project, I asked, how much do you each have to do?

One of my daughter's classmates—someone good at math, I suppose—immediately called out, "Fifty percent." I asked the rest of the class to raise their hands if they thought that was right—

and every hand went up. My response? "Absolutely wrong!" Team-work isn't about each person doing his or her share. It's about everyone doing the most they can, giving 100 percent. Teams generate amazing results when everybody pushes themselves to their limit. That's how victories happen. We each have to own responsibility for the outcome, and take on as much of the bur-den as we can. We each have to look for problems and then solve them, and look for opportunities to take advantage of. We have to treat the challenges of our teammates and coworkers as our challenges, too, and step in to help wherever we are able to. The entire mission belongs to all of us.

When there's competition in a workplace, or on a team—when people have their own agendas, or find themselves sabotaging the efforts of their colleagues, doing poor work, or intentionally or subconsciously making other people's jobs harder—that work-place is seriously broken. There is nothing more important than the team—team, then teammate, then self, I can't repeat it often enough. They drum the lesson into you over and over again as a SEAL. Yet sometimes there are still situations when ego comes into play and self-interest trumps cooperation, and missions suf-fer because of it.

+ + +

When I first arrived in southeastern Afghanistan to lead SEAL Team TWO and our Special Operations Task Force in the re-gion, the situation was less than ideal. There was an infesta-tion of Taliban in the area, with one particular district, Chora, a rural town located in Uruzgan Province with a population of about three thousand, a real hotbed of activity. The main route to Kandahar passed through Chora, and it was an important strategic location to control. But when I arrived, there were no forces there, nothing stopping the Taliban from running wild.

The Colonel in charge of the conventional (non–special ops) forces in the region was less than thrilled when my SEAL Team arrived. We came with energy and conviction, looking for new ideas to improve the situation and ready to move our efforts forward. The Colonel, on the other hand, had been there for a while, and had become accustomed to the status quo. He had cautioned his men and women against taking too much risk, had seemingly accepted that this was an area the Taliban would always control and opted to stay out of their way. Faced with someone who came in wanting to do more, he became a roadblock, standing in my way and in the way of the mission.

Although the Colonel was not in my direct chain of command, we were supposed to work together. Instead, he fought me at every turn. When I wanted to move our SEALs into Chora and set up an outpost there, he didn't want me to use his extra buildings and take advantage of the infrastructure already built. When I wanted to take offensive action to get rid of the Taliban presence in Chora, he said no—and not only refused to help, but asked us not to pursue our efforts, because he didn't want to upset the status quo. My team came up with some extraordinary ways to improve the situation—in both a strategic sense for the overall conflict and also in a very concrete sense for the innocent Afghans living in the area. We built physical barriers—including something we called the Great Wall of Chora, made of wire mesh and canvas flat packs that we filled with sand to make thick barricades—to create choke points and checkpoints to protect the population and keep the Taliban contained. We ended up in gunfights, but we were prepared, we won, and we were able to drive away the Taliban presence to a huge extent.

There had been a girls' school in Chora before the Taliban's arrival. Not long after the Taliban took over the town, the school closed, its classes forced to go underground. It wasn't safe to teach young girls in the area. After we cleared the Taliban out of central Chora, the school was able to reopen. The village elder and the teacher in charge came to us and brought one of my men a basket of fresh fruit as a gift for enabling them to once again teach the girls in safety. None of us had ever received a more meaningful gift.

Throughout my time in the region, I fostered a relationship with the Colonel's superiors in Kandahar, demonstrating strategic alignment and a "one-team" mentality. Our efforts helped them achieve their strategic goals, and we were able to do that with or without the Colonel's help. In many ways, it was an illustration of the very same "leader and follower" point, but at an organizational level, not just an individual one. We, as a SEAL Team, knew that we had to step up and lead here—success wasn't going to be achieved by merely following the wishes of the Colonel and stepping aside. We understood—and got the Colonel's superiors to quickly understand—that letting us be SEALs and execute our plan was going to be the smartest road to achieving the military's goals in the region. By the time the Colonel had left Chora on his regular rotation home, midway through my team's deployment, he had a compromised reputation among the SEALs and among his superiors. He was replaced by another Colonel, with whom we got along wonderfully—and together, our combined efforts were able to make even more significant progress in eliminating the Taliban from the area.

+ + +

That first Colonel was simply never able to get on board with our efforts. He was stuck in his belief that his plan—avoid all risk and sacrifice the chance for progress—was the only plan, and that he was the only one whose ideas were worth listening to. Even when I had gotten support from his superiors to move forward, he could not shift his thinking to support the mission, and he was unwilling to take on any pain in order to help. He was never going to be a follower, and he was never going to make things easier for me and my team. He was never going to be a partner, and from start to finish, his attitude and behavior hurt the overall mission.

I can contrast this with another story, that of a platoon commander named Mark. His platoon was co-located within my Special Operations Task Force headquarters in Tarin Kowt, the birthplace of Mullah Omar, the founder of the Taliban. Mark's team was partnered with an Afghan Special Forces team, and our guys were training the Afghans to take on the risk of leading their own nation. One night, a 25-minute helicopter ride away from Mark's team, another SEAL platoon commander named Andy was leading an offensive mission against known Taliban enemies, trying to clear targets and make the region safer. Andy learned on this night that more Taliban forces were on their way, setting up to attack his team. I knew he needed reinforcements, and although he told me over the radio that he was okay, I had a gut feeling that he soon wouldn't be, and that he needed backup quickly.

I reached out to Mark to let him know the situation, and before I could even finish my first sentence, he was on it. In my role, I had to be aware of everything happening in the two dozen outstations under my command. In Mark's position, his vantage point was more limited. He didn't necessarily know what was happening with Andy's team, and some degree of reluctance, trepidation, or fear would have been, well, human. Instead, at twenty-eight years old, Mark calmly and confidently took ownership of the situation. He immediately got his team together, pulled up Andy's operations plan, studied the terrain, coordinated with supporting ground and air assets, and prepared the mission. As quickly as possible, he became the expert I needed him to be, and his platoon was ready to go the moment Andy confirmed that he could use backup. Out of the helicopter, they helped flank the large number of Taliban and provided necessary assistance to complete the mission. Between Mark's platoon and Andy's platoon, the Taliban fighters were destroyed, and the area was cleared out—without a single scratch on the American troops.

Later, after things had calmed down, I reflected on the night's events, and I realized how much we all owed Andy for taking on such a hard mission, and how much we owed Mark and his team for being so quick and willing to calmly and smartly take on mortal risk, get on a helicopter, and land in the middle of a gunfight. They embodied the idea that the more you hurt, the less your teammates hurt—and in this case, they were able to make it so that no one on our side ended up hurt at all.

We all have to do what we can to make the lives of those around us easier, not harder. That's how we create a cohesive environment and turn people into true partners. That's how we win. Even when we're not talking about life-or-death gunfights, we can all try to step up when others need us, and aim to take things off people's plates instead of piling on more weight for others to carry. We can become leaders when the situation is asking for us to lead—and in the process, build real relationships founded on truth and trust. When working in a situation where I can absorb some of a leader's burdens—whether in the military, the White House, or in business—I've tried to divide the tasks we perform into three categories: what I can do that my boss doesn't even need to think about, what I can do that I can tell my boss about later, and what I absolutely need to tell my boss about now to make sure we are on the same page. The more I can put in those first two categories and not take up his or her time in the moment, the better off the organization is.

Mark went on to become a White House Fellow, and I can't wait to see how the rest of his career unfolds. I know him as someone truly able to step up when needed, and to be flexible and agile as situations change and develop. These are qualities we can all build in ourselves, no matter the roles we play.

Everyone Works for You, You Work for Everyone

You probably don't expect to hear this from someone who spent two decades in the US military, an organization not exactly known for its disregard of rank and title—but the truth is that at any given moment, on any particular mission, hierarchy doesn't and shouldn't matter. If hierarchy is getting in the way of the best decision being made, or precluding the best person from taking on any particular role, then something is deeply wrong. At every point along the way, you want your strongest team on the field, and you want people stepping forward and stepping back based on their competencies, not their titles.

The person first on a scene—or the first to notice a problem, just to broaden us out from the military world—should be the first one who thinks about how it can potentially get worse, and what kind of response network needs to be activated. That means you don't approach a situation assuming that it's someone else's concern or, as you hear people say sometimes, "it's above my pay grade."

That's never the right kind of thinking. Nothing is above—or below—anyone's pay grade. The most junior person should be thinking about big-picture strategy if he or she has something useful to contribute, and just as critically, the most senior person shouldn't think anything going on in the organization is beneath him or her—and truly, a leader who knows what's happening on the ground is always going to be able to apply that knowledge toward making better decisions at the top of the organization. There are absolutely reasons why, just as an example, you may not want the CEO to carry his own bags to and from the train station—perhaps it's more useful to keep his hands free to use those ten minutes to make calls to clients—but the idea that he's too important, too special, or too senior to do it shouldn't be on the list.

Fundamentally, seniority shouldn't be dictating decisions. What matters is if the decision is right, not who makes the decision. The higher up you are in an organization, the more you need to understand that it's not your job to make the best decision—your job is to ensure the best decision gets made. You need to be able to identify the best people to make the decision, and be open to listening to everyone up and down the hierarchy, because you never know how the best answer will emerge.

Ego too often gets in the way here. People with powerful

titles—or people who seek those titles—are frequently afraid not to be the ones seen making decisions. We feel we have to justify our role by making the important calls ourselves, or we think we'll be seen as dispensable if we're not the ones with the big idea. Being the one with the big idea is great—unless someone else had an even better idea that you pushed aside in your race to get the credit. When we're insecure about our role, our standing, or our importance—that's when we hunt for credit and think we need to prove something to anyone who's watching. When we're comfortable with who we are and what we bring to the table, we're unafraid to share the spotlight, unbothered by other people being celebrated, unselfish about praise. We realize, when we're secure, that the organization's success is our success, and we all rise and fall as one.

+ + +

Reed was twenty-three years old, just out of training, when he was on my team. I had been spending time trying to advance what was known as the "power problem." Getting electric power to outstations throughout a war zone is a huge challenge. While "green energy" wasn't exactly a concept embraced by the military from an environmental perspective—the immediate needs do tend to push longer-term issues to the side—I saw clear battle-field benefits if we could harness alternative energy sources. Anything to be lighter, be more capable or durable, reduce risk, or save money is in the interest of the overall mission. As an example, traditionally we often use helicopters to drop countless tons of diesel to power generators that must run 24 hours a day, 7 days a week. This is not ideal, nor is the use of expensive con-tracted trucks to deliver diesel, traveling on incredibly risky roads to do so. When we do have to use helicopters, we do so reluctantly, because helicopters are valuable assets. Using them to airdrop gasoline means we can't use them for transporting troops to missions or evacuating injured men and women to safety. There is also risk to the pilots and to people on the ground every time there is a fuel drop. Plus, there ends up being a 3-hour window where people have to wait for fuel, instead of doing whatever else could be done for the mission at hand. Finally, the fuel is costly and often wasted: since the generators have to run 24/7 and are typically sized for the maximum necessary load, the vast majority of the electricity they produce often goes unused.

Admiral Philip Cullom is a highly distinguished (now retired) Naval officer who was leading the charge at the time for green energy solutions for the entire US Navy. His task was not easy. In the military, there is often real tension between laboratories in the Pentagon (or elsewhere) dreaming up breakthrough ideas to advance modern warfare and support and field units only wanting to use a new development if it has already been combat-tested. It takes forward-thinking units to be willing to simultaneously be in combat and test new things. So even though Cullom and his team had developed several potential solutions to the power problem, it was challenging to get them off the ground.

One of these solutions came from a company that had used new technology to link a battery bank to their generators, enabling field units to store power that would otherwise have gone to waste. This meant the generators no longer needed to run anywhere close to 24 hours a day, a lot less gas was consumed, many fewer helicopter hours were flown, and incredible amounts of money and time were saved.

I needed someone to help me think about technologies like these, figure out which we were interested in and able to test, and how we would do it without adding burden or increasing risk to the troops. I identified something in Reed that made me think he would understand and be excited by the challenge (not every SEAL was thinking about the power problem, or would even care, to be honest). And within a week of bringing him on board, he had become an expert, learning far more about the mechanics of energy and the range of new technologies out there than I ever would. Reed had great ideas and strategic insights about everything from solar to windmills to waterfalls.

I brought Reed with me to meet Admiral Cullom in his Pentagon office. It's not every day that a rookie officer—Reed was an ensign, an O1 rank at the time, the most junior an officer could be—gets an audience with an Admiral, but I trusted Reed and knew he would make a good impression. For Admiral Cullom, this was a win-win situation. To be able to share that the SEALs were on board with new green energy initiatives was a coup for him—if something is good enough for the SEALs, then surely it's good enough for the rest of the Navy. Cullom wanted me to follow up by coming to Washington and briefing the Secretary of the Navy on our efforts. I would have 20 minutes alone with the Secretary to tell him what we were doing, and how it was paving the way for a solution to the power problem going forward.

I told Admiral Cullom that I didn't need to be in the room with the Secretary—Reed had become the expert, and Reed should do the briefing alone. I knew that because of the military hierarchy, Reed wouldn't have felt like he could take the lead if I was in the room, too. And I knew it would make a much bigger impact on the Secretary to have a brand-new officer telling him about power strategy within the SEALs than to have me doing it. Indeed, the feedback I got after the session was that they talked for much longer than 20 minutes, and that the Secretary was blown away by how confident an expert Reed was, and how much good the SEALs were doing in the energy arena—not just for show, but in terms of real, combat-oriented efforts.

+ + +

Sometimes the best thing is for the new guy to be the one in charge—both for the new guy and for the organization as a whole. I happily enabled Reed to look like a star, and Reed made us all look good. Why shouldn't he have had the privilege of taking the lead? The lesson is partly about not being afraid to let the most junior person on the team take the reins, but it's also about not even thinking about someone's rank or seniority as a factor in what they can learn or do. If Reed had been at my level instead of an O1, but was in the best position to be the expert about green energy, then he still should have been the one in the room with the Secretary. Our knowledge, passion, and ability matters—not our position in the hierarchy.

It goes the other way, too. As Commander, I would sometimes go on missions with my teams, partly to observe them in action, partly to keep up my skills and comfort in combat, and partly because it's important for a leader to be willing to take on the same risk he's asking his people to take on. In some scenarios, these missions could be uncomfortable for the rest of the team—it's like any situation when the boss is suddenly around where he typically isn't. Everyone else might feel a little more guarded, a little less open. I tried hard not to make my team feel that way.

There was a running joke among the SEALs that some "strap-hangers," or people not fighting nightly in the SEAL platoon, would try to go out on a single mission so they could qualify for an award or two, while the real operators were going out night after night. So whenever I walked into the room on a night that I was going out with the guys, I'd just tell them, "Fellas, I've already written my award for heroism for tonight. Now we just have to go out and do the mission!" I knew (and they knew) that I wasn't really needed. They could absolutely do their mission without me.

On these missions, I'd plan to be the guy most out of the way, in the back, with the command-and-control element—usually the next most senior officer and the radio guy. Of course, on the ground, the back can quickly become the front. On one particular mission when I went out with the guys in Iraq, we had planned to take down an insurgent cell known to be located in three or four buildings in a village overrun with Sunni extremists. I was one of four SEALs on the outskirts, making sure the area was clear before establishing the command-and-control position. Suddenly, through my grainy, green night-vision goggles, I saw a family—a mom, a dad, a ten-year-old kid, and a baby—sleeping outside a shack on a 2-foot-high platform. This wasn't entirely unusual; given the middle-of-the-night heat in Iraq, families often slept outside. But something about this situation felt off to me. Twenty-one feet, we learn in training, is a magic number. If someone starts to pull a gun on you and you're unarmed and within 21 feet of them, you are actually better off running toward them than running away, because you can potentially reach them before they can reach their weapon. I was about 20 feet away when I noticed the family (but of course, in this case, I had my rifle and pistol on me). I saw the father start to reach for something. Instinct told me this was bad.

I spoke firmly and clearly to the guy behind me, calling his name—"Joel, Joel, Joel"—so he would know that I was about to make a move and could cover me, and I held the Iraqi man in my crosshairs, ready to shoot him at any moment, as I rushed as fast as I could toward him before he could grab what did turn out to be a weapon. He was reaching for an AK rifle just as I put my foot on his arm so he wouldn't be able to point the weapon at me or any of my teammates. Then I quickly put my muzzle on his chest and subdued him, and enlisted Joel's help to properly detain him with flex cuffs (plastic handcuffs). I could have shot him at any time, but as I first approached him, I didn't know for sure that he was armed, and my instant and instinctive calculation made me confident that I would be fast enough to get to him before he could take a shot at me or anyone else if he did have a weapon.

It turned out that the AK was fully loaded and he had three magazines . . . and after we got him cuffed, his family under our control, and our targets secured, we realized through our interrogation process that he was in fact the number two most wanted enemy in western Iraq at the time. "Anytime you need something done," I joked (loudly and obnoxiously) to my team afterward, "just ask the officer." Of course, we all knew it was pure luck that had put me in the position to subdue him. Everyone else on the team would have done exactly the same. The other guys had captured literally hundreds, if not thousands, of more dangerous insurgents and terrorists than I had. But it hammered home the lesson that anyone can be the lead actor at any given time. We dynamically adjust based on the situation. We rewrite the map.

+ + +

I would regularly emphasize to the newest and most junior SEAL that on any given operation, he could find himself in the front, with the best vantage point and plan, and how it would be his job to step up and tell people what he needed them to do— but I would also remind the most experienced SEALs on my team that tonight might be their night as well. Anyone can be the leader at any time. Being able to react to current situations on the ground is not easy, and of course you always need to make sure there aren't multiple teammates trying to go in different directions, turning the situation into anarchy and undirected chaos. That's where training comes in, but it's also a place where attitude and expectations play a huge role. If no one expects to automatically be in charge based on position or seniority, then it's far easier to give up control when you see that someone else is better positioned to lead in the moment.

How you create an organization that can support this kind of dynamic subordination—this constant forward and backward movement—is a cultural issue, and depends on the kind of organization-level agility we'll talk more about in chapter 6. But on an individual level, it means you must always be prepared to take the reins, and just as prepared to hand them off. Great leaders must know how to lead and how to follow, but most important, they have to know when to do which. That's what differentiates them from the rest of the pack. In the business world, I've spoken about this issue to two different top-five banks, explaining that in a crisis, they didn't need to have a playbook—because every situation is always going to play out differently, and we can never know all the details in advance.

They needed to have a meta-playbook, a plan for making the playbook on the fly, for people moving forward and back and enabling great leaders to step up.

(Of course, when I say "great leaders," I don't mean just the people at the top of the hierarchy—I mean everyone. Because if there's one point I'm trying to make here, it's that everyone is a leader—or at least they're only one moment away from finding themselves in the circumstances where they ought to become one.)

The SEAL mindset is fundamentally one where you see yourself with the power and ability to control things that most people believe are uncontrollable, while at the same time having the humility not to force your own way on the world. Everyone can work for you, but you also have to be willing and eager to work for everyone.

Succeed at Your Assigned Mission, Not the Mission You Want

There is inevitably unpleasant work to be done on any SEAL mission. There are people who have to hide themselves on a roof for three days in extreme heat with limited water, in order to watch for anything that might be going on in the town below. In those long, slow hours, you find yourself counting the bugs around you, studying the environment, playing card games without the actual cards. You know that at any given moment, things could turn messy and you could find yourself in the middle of a gunfight—but until that point, it's just boredom. Not every job feels meaningful at every point along the way—although the best leaders will connect even the smallest tasks to the larger mission and make everyone understand how they are valuable (and valued) parts of the team. Bigger picture, not everyone always agrees with every mission. There are going to be choices made that each of us may have decided differently, benchmarks we don't believe are the right ones, strategies we don't fully trust or understand. We can and should push back against them, but sometimes we fail, and then we find ourselves on a mission we don't fully connect with, or playing a role we don't truly want to play.

And then there are times that you can be tempted to bring your organization on a mission that turns out to be selfish, and isn't in the best interest of the team. From the first day of military training, you learn that securing your weapon is critical. You lose your weapon, it's like losing a limb. We had a guy, a senior enlisted, who was typically an excellent performer, a team player, and everything you want in a partner, who lost his pistol at one point. He realized it must have fallen out while he was in the door of a helicopter the previous night as part of a quick reaction force. This team would routinely fly a preplanned distance around a target, waiting in reserve in case an ongoing mission went sideways, ready to get called quickly into action at high speed and at a high angle. I found out the next day that he was trying to get his team to repeat the previous night's mission and go out in the same general area so he could look for his missing gun.

I was furious when I heard about this. How could he risk the lives of his teammates on an unnecessary mission simply because he wanted to avoid looking like he was irresponsible and careless? You can never let your own personal desires distort the decision-making process. The truth is that while it's never acceptable to lose your weapon, it's even less acceptable to put your team at risk. In this particular situation, it wasn't like the guy just dropped his weapon on his way to breakfast and didn't know where it was. To go back and search an active battlefield is an incredibly poor decision. Obviously not all situations have this kind of life-or-death stakes, but that he would consider putting people at risk when it wasn't absolutely necessary was shocking and upsetting to me, far more upsetting than the fact that he had lost his weapon in the first place.

In another situation, someone smuggled a dog out of the combat zone. We are not supposed to bring animals out of the field, for the same reason that international travelers aren't supposed to bring home plants or produce of any kind: we don't want to introduce nonnative species or diseases back in the US. But this soldier had fallen in love with a stray dog, and at the end of his deployment, he snuck it onto the plane in his bag. The flight landed back in the US, the customs agent boarded, and the dog was found . . . which meant that the whole entry process for everyone on the plane had to come to a stop. The dog had to be quarantined, examined, and given its shots, and for everyone else on the plane, that meant hours of waiting. Normally we think of extra hours in the airport as an annoying inconvenience, but in this case, these were men and women who had just spent months away from their loved ones in service to their country and were finally getting to go home and see them. Adding hours to their long-awaited and much-deserved reunions felt pretty unconscionable to me.

✦ ✦ ✦

These were not hard cases. These were rules or norms that deserved to be in place, and the people causing problems were, in those moments, bad actors. (We all have our moments of

poor judgment, for sure, but we should aim to minimize them.)
Where the situations get harder is when there are rules that you
truly believe deserve to be broken, or where your organization
may not be on the mission you'd like it to be. I'd be lying if I said
there were always easy answers. You do what you can to change
an organization, and to move a team in the right direction. But
in the moment, you have to play your role, and you have to be
the best team member you can be. I've certainly stepped into
roles that weren't my first choice, to help out the greater mission
and fill a gap that needed to be filled. We owe it to our organizations to try our best to understand and connect with their
missions, and then do what makes the organization better, not
what makes us feel the best.

An Individual Can Fail—An Organization Can't

We have to have room for people to fail. Whenever we are being pushed to our maximum capacity, doing hard things, facing
uncomfortable situations, extending the limits of what we think
we are capable of, there will always be a chance of failure at the
individual level. That's okay—if we never fail, we're clearly not
pushing ourselves hard enough. But a good organization sets
itself up so that the failure of an individual does not mean the
failure of the organization. Other people have to step forward
when one person falls back.

I remember a situation during a reconnaissance mission
where my team snowshoed in subzero temperatures. During the
day, we were hiding in brutal conditions along the steep slope of
a mountain. One of my teammates, Danny, a superb SEAL, was
horribly sick with a virus during this ordeal. We were all miser-

able, but Danny, fighting a high fever and looking like someone who ought to be home in bed, was clearly much worse off than the rest of us. Seeing what terrible shape he was in, I approached him and told him that we could cancel the mission if he needed us to, and I was fully open to that possibility. It was not worth risking his life to complete the mission, which was to confirm or deny the presence of illicit activity at one particular site in one random three-day window.

Danny, sick as he was, refused to let us quit. He refused to let the team down, no matter how he felt. Danny looked at me and said that as long as we could deal with him stepping back and not taking his turns "on the glass" (looking through binoculars and other optical equipment), he could absolutely deal with his misery on his own and suffer in silence. He was not willing to be the reason we couldn't complete the task.

Most people would have gladly taken me up on my offer to quit, especially if they were in the condition Danny was obviously in. But even though he knew he wasn't in a position to step up and lead, or even to do his assigned job, he didn't want to bring us down.

Fortunately, we had others who could step in and take his place, and Danny's calculation in this particular situation was right: we had sufficient manpower, and sufficient agility, to let him fail. We could support him and keep the mission going without suffering as an organization. (Of course, if Danny had needed medical attention, or if his condition had gotten worse, we would have absolutely aborted the mission to get him the help he needed. Same thing if I had felt his diminished capability was going to put us at any increased risk. It was only because Danny was so insistent that he could handle it—and because I knew he would be honest with me if he couldn't—that I contin-ued the mission.)

Sometimes the best thing we can do is let someone else take the reins, whether we're sick or, more often, we simply realize that someone else is better positioned to bring us success. But the lesson of this chapter isn't really to step back, at least not often. The lesson is to step up, whenever you can, to make your life and the lives of those around you better. Being ready to do whatever is needed at any given moment is what makes the world stronger. If we think about tragedies that we read about in the news each day, there are often heroes who step forward and end up saving lives. The definition of a hero, in a lot of people's eyes, is just an ordinary person who steps up to do something extraordinary. These are people who didn't wake up that morning expecting to lead, but when circumstances presented themselves, they did, and others ended up so much better off for it. We only have to look at the opposite situations—times when no one steps up and outcomes turn out worse—to know how true that really is.

This is no less relevant for slow-moving issues, whether it's local governmental policies or budget decisions in any organiza-tion. There are things we disagree with, or that can be done bet-ter, but that no one is sufficiently acting upon. If we see ourselves as capable of leading, or sometimes following, even when no one is asking us to, we can exert far more power than we realize, and change the world for the better.

+ + +

As you see from these lessons, agility is key when it comes to the roles we all play. We have to be able to move forward and move back in a dynamic process, based on ever-changing circumstances. Sometimes we lead and sometimes we follow. Sometimes we're the ones making the important decisions—and sometimes we have to either delegate or accept that the decision is not ours to make, and then do the best we can with the plan that has been put in place.

But the next chapter is about the decisions that we own, the choices we *are* empowered to make, either for ourselves or for our teams and organizations. When I ran SEAL Team TWO, we spent months with at least one unit in direct combat with the Taliban, and sometimes more than five units were in gunfights at the same time. We didn't harm anyone we shouldn't have. Why? Luck, certainly, but also an agile decision-making process. That process is the piece I want to turn to next.

CHAPTER 5

LEARN HOW TO THINK, NOT WHAT TO THINK

Agility in the Decisions You Make

I opened the introduction to this book with a story from 2007, in Fallujah, Iraq. A smart and experienced SEAL named Josh and I were faced with an Iraqi man who stepped out of a house, reached into his clothing, and—do we shoot, or not? Each of us made the independent decision not to, and it was a good thing we didn't, because he was an innocent man reaching for his ID card, not, in fact, the terrorist threat we knew he might have been.

In these kinds of situations in the military, we're governed only by our training and the rules of engagement (ROE). The ROE is a military code that tells you when you can use deadly force. The goal of national security is never to be in these situations, to never need to take a life. But there Josh and I were, and the rules of engagement say that if you believe you are being threatened with deadly force, you are authorized to shoot.

Whether to shoot was a different decision, however, and it was one we each had to make on our own. My status as the senior officer made zero difference here—in these moments, no SEAL has to stop to ask for permission or advice about what to do.

We were ready to shoot—but, as I said in the introduction, Josh and I were each confident that we had enough time to wait and see what the man did with that hand in his robe, and that this was more than a binary yes/no decision. With less training, less confidence, less ability to think effectively in the moment, the situation would have played out like a simple algorithm: Is there every indication of a deadly threat? Absolutely. So you have to remove that threat, and shoot so you and your team don't get hurt. You end up safe, every time, but that innocent Iraqi, not so much.

Seeing your choices as mutually exclusive like that, seeing a situation as forcing you to pick one option or the other, is an approach that, to me, is a kind of binary thinking I call "what to think." Deadly force? Shoot. No time for complications, no reason to wonder if there might be a few more milliseconds of flexibility to ask yourself any further questions.

But having a true thought process, considering the bigger picture, having confidence about the elements of a situation that you can control, realizing that the best decisions don't just follow a simple algorithm but actually involve a consideration of the principles layered on top of the rules, and the specific circumstances of the situation—that's not a "what to think" situation.

Josh knew this wasn't necessarily a black-and-white decision. He didn't ask himself, "Can I shoot?" He asked himself, "*Should* I shoot?" And his judgment told him not to, not yet. Because he had learned not just *what* to think, but *how* to think. He had learned how, in making the best decisions, we need to think about more than just the "yes" and the "no." We need to think about the "why."

+ + +

In our debrief after the mission, I called out Josh's behavior for the rest of my team, shining a light on Josh's process so that everyone would better understand what I expected from each of them. The details ultimately didn't matter—who the man was, how far we were from the door, etc. It was the thought process that was important. After every operation, the team would debrief, and we would talk about what happened and what we could have done better—the true, honest feedback I talked about in chapter 1.

But whenever the discussion started to turn to specifics—we turned left, we went through the door, we zigged, we zagged—I would stop and remind my team that we're never going to be in the exact same situation a second time, so the decisions themselves—the "what"—don't matter. It's the "why" and the "how" we have to think about. Why did you make that decision? How did you balance all of the factors you were considering? Those are the questions that are going to be applicable next time, when the specific circumstances will almost certainly look entirely different. Those are the questions that ultimately lead to a system that produces good decisions, time and time again, for ourselves and for our organizations—with as few errors as possible. Those are the questions that help make us agile enough to decide correctly on the fly even as circumstances change.

+ + +

This idea—that we need to worry about how to think, not what to think—means the decision-making process you have in place is far more important for advance planning than the decisions themselves. You never know in advance what the precise situation is going to be, or how it's going to change while you're in it. The secret to the success of the SEALs is our agility, our ability to adjust on the fly, our deeply embedded process of reacting and replanning in the moment as conditions shift.

On any given operation, we plan for multiple contingencies. For example, we make it a point to establish helicopter landing zones on all sides of any target so we can decide at the very last second which is the safest and best place to get picked back up. Helmuth von Moltke, a nineteenth-century Prussian general who helped forge the unification of Germany in the 1870s, famously said, "No plan of operations extends with any certainty beyond the first contact with the main hostile force." (This is often paraphrased as "No plan survives contact with the enemy.") Moltke's saying simply isn't true in the SEALs. Our plan, from the very start, is for our initial plan not to survive that first contact with the enemy—so we're already planning to replan. We're a step ahead of Moltke, and so is any agile business, team, or individual.

Ultimately, the right process—one that allows you to plan and replan quickly and successfully—is what gives you the greatest chance for success. In over a thousand decisions about whether to launch an air-to-ground engagement with the enemy in Afghanistan, my team never harmed anyone we shouldn't have. There were times we didn't drop a bomb on a building, and on the video feed afterward, we'd see women and children walking out of that building. Thank goodness we made the choice not to engage, because we could have killed innocent families.

We spent over four months in direct combat with the Taliban, and remarkably, we were the only Task Force not to lose an American life or hurt any innocent parties on the other side. Were we lucky to have an error rate of zero? Maybe. Probably. But I'd like to think it was more than luck. It was our process. We had two dozen outstations in my region, each one with roughly ten to fifteen special operations forces, and about the same number of supporting personnel stationed with them. Some locations were impossible to get to by land, and we would have to helicopter in all food and supplies; some didn't have running water. I couldn't be everywhere at once to make those life-or-death decisions. I had to rely on the people working with me.

The way I did that was to first give them guidelines. For one thing, if they were asking to drop a bomb on a building where a civilian, American or otherwise, might be inside, they shouldn't even be asking the question. It's not the right thing to do, it will do more harm than good, don't even waste my time. Guidelines like that went a long way, but still wouldn't get the error rate down to zero. How you get to zero requires more. In that spirit, there are five principles that I use to define my decision-making process, to guide me when setting up how to think about a problem and how to arrive at the best answer. In the rest of this chapter, I'll walk you through each of those principles.

All High-Stakes Decisions Are Fundamentally the Same

I hear the question all the time: "How did you manage to move from the military to the government to the private sector, when those arenas are so different from each other?" My answer is to challenge the premise of the question. Of course there are different details, different specifics, but the truth is, in my experience, all high-stakes organizations and all high-stakes decisions are pretty much the same. The concrete knowledge you need is the easy part—anyone can learn that. But the details don't matter if you don't have the right process. And if you do have the right process, you can go anywhere. It's why strong leaders are able to jump from one industry to another, one organization to another.

It goes back to my story about the White House Fellows, and being in the room with one of the most senior leaders in the administration, telling him I didn't know a thing about START. He and I both realized that didn't matter, because I had the skills to get the right people engaged in the room and motivated to come together toward agreement. And those are the skills that matter. Those are the "how to think" skills, not the "what to think" details that too often drive people's opinions about whether someone is the right fit for a particular role.

When I'm making decisions about people—whether in a hiring process or deploying people for a particular task at a particular time—I keep in mind that someone with great intrinsic skills can be put in charge of anything and they will figure it out. Past experience doing exactly the same task is barely relevant, because no meaningful task will ever turn out exactly the same the next time. There will be complications, new information, twists and turns that you can't predict—and so you need someone with the agility and ability to effectively change course.

The world doesn't always see it this way. There's a difference between substance and perception. Perception is what the world thinks of you, but substance is what you truly have inside. I wasn't necessarily perceived as the right person to lead the nuclear treaty discussions, but the leader in charge felt I had the substance that mattered. I kept that in mind when I chose Reed to help me solve the energy problem for the SEALs (as I described in chapter 4), and I've kept it in mind whenever I've chosen people for new roles and opportunities.

Get the Broadest Range of Inputs Possible

In Afghanistan, I slept in a bed 50 feet away from my operations center and had a red police-style light mounted to the ceiling directly above me. This was so my "watch officer"—a critical leadership position staffed 24/7—could awaken me at the flip of a switch from down the hall. When the red light came on, I would sprint to the ops center—where even a second could end up being the difference between life and death. I got to the point where I would wake up to a sound the light made milliseconds before the bulb even lit up.

No matter how little sleep I had, I needed to instantly be switched on mentally and locked into the situation at hand. Being woken up at three in the morning to make a life-or-death decision, frequently in less than 60 seconds, was something I couldn't get wrong. What I wanted—needed—in that moment was someone next to me who saw things completely differently from me, who could stress test my thinking, see the things I wouldn't see. Literally, our heads can turn to see 250 degrees of a circle—but we need someone else to see the other 110.

Ultimately, responsibility for the decisions rested on me, but I wanted to know I was doing everything I could to cover my blind spots. (Because we all have blind spots, and if you believe you don't—well, there you go. I've found your blind spot.) I made sure to have people close to me with a range of experiences and expertise, from a military lawyer to a young officer just out of training.

+ + +

I needed people around me with a range of experiences because what you need in any decision-making process is the broadest diversity of thought you can possibly get. That's why prioritizing inclusion is so critical—all the things that make us different provide the range of perspectives and points of view we absolutely need whenever we're making decisions.

As humans, we naturally gravitate toward people who are like us. We get excited to find common ground. When we meet someone who grew up in a situation we recognize, who went to the same high school or college as we did, or had similar life experiences, we are inclined to have favorable feelings toward them, to bond with them, and to want to be around them. Artists like spending time with artists. Engineers like spending time with engineers. But if you want what's best for a decision-making system, you need the artist paired up with the engineer, because each is going to see a situation differently. There are people who are great at generating ideas. There are people who are great at building things. There are people who are great at execution. You need all those people, every time you make a decision. Biodiversity ensures the survival of a species. Same thing for a company or organization: none of us, no matter how talented, can do everything.

I've found over time that lots of people give lip service to the idea of diversity, but they don't truly believe in it. Valuing diversity really does mean that you can appreciate ideas and perspectives that aren't the same as yours. If we believe that hearing different viewpoints and lived experiences leads to better decisions—and we must—then we have to trust the process and be comfortable even when things don't go our way. People think it's bad to have friction in an organization. They want harmony, above all else. But the tension of competing ideas makes an organization stronger.

What that means is that we have to be welcoming of others who don't share our views, and who may disagree fundamentally. In fact, we have to celebrate those differences. And diversity of thought doesn't just mean having all these different kinds of people in the room—it means genuinely listening to them, and having a culture and a process where everyone's voices are heard and respected. It has to be a place where ideas can be comfortably and securely presented. Even if you've done an amazing job of hiring people who are not like you in every possible way, who reflect all the different elements of diversity that we have in our world, and you have all these diverse thinkers at your fingertips, if you're the one running the process, you also need to make sure you've created a culture where people feel comfortable speaking up, telling you what they really think, and trusting you are not only open to their input but that you need it, that it's a must-have.

There are many different ways to complete a SEAL mission. In some cases, we would make decisions about how to approach a target. Do we drive up in an armored vehicle, visible to all, then quickly jump out and hit that target, relying on our speed and agility? Or do we take a helicopter, land a few miles away, and walk silently, undetected, to maintain the element of surprise? There could be arguments on both sides, legitimate cases to be made. When we were ready to go, thirty of us outside in the desert in 130-degree heat, exhausted, it was easy to imagine that twenty-one-year-old new SEAL on his first mission seeing something that concerned him, but afraid to speak up. That's a failure of an organization. That kid might have been seeing something no one else was—and he needs to know that speaking up isn't just okay, it's required and welcomed.

Besides, people knowing a leader is listening to their ideas helps gain buy-in for whatever the decision might be. If you know your idea was invited, heard, and considered, then even if it wasn't chosen, at least you feel like a respected part of the process. And that's critical in maintaining spirits and making everyone feel like a valuable part of the team. If you smack ideas down, then the good ones will never bubble up. Of course, there will be situations when you don't have time to listen to every idea— but if the team knows that your default is to hear from them, the exceptions are understandable and don't destroy morale.

+ + +

After leaving the SEALs, my first job in the private sector was at Bridgewater Associates, the world's largest and most successful hedge fund. I worked as Chief of Staff to the CEO and then in a Chief Operating Officer role. The firm had (and still has) an incredible collection of human capital, many of the smartest people I've ever met. It was built by founder Ray Dalio to be an idea meritocracy, where contributions at even the highest level can come from anyone at the firm—as long as they can be explained with complete, impeccable logic.

Bridgewater has gotten attention for its culture of assertiveness and intensity, but that passion is in pursuit of uncovering the best ideas and training employees to think as rigorously as possible. At Bridgewater, everything has to be explained in terms of data, logic, and synthesis—are you looking at the right information, are you applying the right thinking to it, and is it leading you to the right decision? When you listen to enough people trying to present their ideas in this form, you and others quickly spot strengths and weaknesses, and can form a good picture of who someone is as a thinker. In turn, you can put together teams of diverse contributors who each bring certain skills to the table. One person might be great at idea generation but struggle with follow-through. One person might be an operational star but only when executing on the ideas of others. One person might be a whiz at finance, but fail to see the ambiguities of the human beings behind the numbers. None of these people should necessarily be making decisions on their own—none of us should be making important decisions completely on our own, really—but together, they can form an unbeatable team.

After I had spent six months at Bridgewater, in a room full of the firm's most senior executives, Ray Dalio posed a question for discussion: "We've all gotten to know Mike. What's he good at, and what's he bad at?" It was scary how well he was able to describe me—my values, my abilities, and my skills. When you're paying attention, in the pursuit of creating the most diverse, balanced, effective team, you can pick up on so much. I learned an entire vocabulary for discussing how people's minds work: conceptual, granular, lateral, linear, left-brain, right-brain. I learned how to build more diverse, effective teams wherever I go. I've often said that we're the average of the people we spend time with—and at a place filled with brilliant individuals like Bridgewater, it's impossible not to be pulled up.

Emphasize the Signal Over the Noise

In Afghanistan, my team had only five dedicated satellite communications channels for our two dozen or so outstations. This meant that every communication needed to be critical—or you risked blocking a transmission that might be needed to save a life. If a sixth unit needed to talk—to ask for backup, to let me know they needed air support, to get someone medevaced, or anything else that required my urgent attention—we would end up with more than one unit needing to share a channel, which was very challenging, since only one voice could come through at any given time. The last thing I wanted was for anyone to waste a channel with needless chatter.

This communication limit could have been seen as an obstacle to effective communication in the field, but in reality, in most cases it simply amplified what was already a critical need to be brief and conserve all our bandwidth for only the most important issues. I told my platoons in the field that they should only communicate on the network if they needed me to make an immediate decision about something, or if they needed to give me information that was going to affect a decision currently being made. If what they were going to say didn't fall into either of those categories, they didn't need to talk to me.

This meant that I didn't know some of what was happening on the ground, at least not at the moment it was happening. When there was no decision I needed to make, merely knowing the information would simply have served to satisfy my curiosity, and that wasn't a high enough bar. My curiosity was only going to degrade the mission. The opportunity cost was high: having to tell me what was happening was only going to take someone's bandwidth and focus away from the situation at hand. The communication limits forced us to have real clarity about what was essential and what was not.

This operational tightness and discipline translates directly to the business world. Again, it's something I learned at Bridgewater. We started every meeting asking what the meeting was intended to accomplish. Were we there to make a decision, to discuss an issue to make sure there was a common understanding, to learn from an internal or external expert being brought in to teach, or to brainstorm to creatively solve a problem? Those were really the only four possible reasons for a meeting—otherwise, we were just talking for the sake of talking. In the private sector, where time is money, you don't want people just talking for the sake of talking—meetings need to have a reason, and the ratio of signal to noise has to be really, really high.

Everyone at Bridgewater needed to leave a meeting with clarity about what task to do next, or what to change about their behavior going forward—otherwise, we could have (and should have) spent that time doing something else. This imperative kept meetings focused, which I think was a very good thing.

This idea of brevity in communications came back to me recently when I heard my friend Chris Cassidy speaking at a prelaunch party for his third trip into space. He talked about how people who know him well know that he values brevity, and it got me thinking: Was that a Chris thing, or a SEAL thing? I think it comes back to the idea mentioned in chapter 1 about the L in SEAL standing for "lazy." We don't want to waste our time. We don't want to fill our lives with noise. We want the most important pieces of information for the decisions we have to make, and then we want to move forward, make the decision, and get to the next one. It's crucial on the battlefield, and just as vital in the boardroom.

The First Decision Is When to Make the Decision

Obviously, this principle was critical as Josh and I decided whether to shoot the Iraqi man in the doorway—but it's always critical. Sometimes people come to you and say that something has to be decided in two minutes, or even less, and other times people say you have two weeks, or maybe longer. Those impulses aren't always the right ones. How do you really know how much time you have to make any particular decision?

For me, it's a simple graph: on one axis is the value of the information you have on hand to help make the decision, and on the other axis is time. If I'm deciding whether to drop a bomb on a building, I might have thirty seconds to gather as much information as I can—any information I gather after that is useless, because our plane can't stay on station any longer, the enemy has moved too close to our forces to safely drop, the opportunity for a clean strike is gone, there are perhaps other critical situations in the vicinity causing a competition for limited airborne resources, or any one of a host of other possible reasons why the moment of importance has passed.

But if I'm deciding where to construct the next headquarters for an organization, it might be months of data-gathering before reaching the inflection point where it's more valuable to go ahead and decide with the information we have than to wait for some additional marginally helpful pieces of knowledge. At some point, the additional value of more information will not be worth the cost of waiting for it. That's when you make the decision.

To a lot of people, that doesn't sound practical. How do you know when you've reached that inflection point? To some extent, it takes practice, and that practice helps to refine your intuition. Intuition is all about unconscious pattern matching, noticing something now that you've seen in the past, and being able to connect the dots and draw conclusions without necessarily having the data. You know you're ready to make the decision, because you've made decisions before and seen how they work out, or don't. But thinking about the decision in these terms—value of information versus time—pushes you to do two things.

First, it forces you to understand the cost of making the decision over time. Is there a point at which the graph takes off and it becomes much costlier to have not made the decision already? You can spend a lot of time thinking about fire safety. Then, all of a sudden, there's a fire. If you're going to wait much longer to pick an escape route, that needs to be some impossibly valuable information you're still waiting for.

Second, it pushes you to get the best information as quickly as you can. What's going to be the most impactful piece of knowledge you could use, and what can you do to speed its acquisition? If you can figure that out, that's where your energy needs to be. Whether it's dropping bombs or making paper clips, there are some bits of information that are going to be the most valuable ones available. Who's in the building? Who's selling the cheapest steel wire? Whatever the information is, how can you get it as quickly and accurately as possible?

Sometimes you can't get it, because the information is unknowable, and you just need to make your best guess. When I was leading my team in Afghanistan, at every outstation we had the capacity to treat injured troops, but not an unlimited capacity to do so. At any given time, we usually had ten units of blood in the blood bank at my headquarters. We got the blood from the main hospital in Kandahar, about a 45-minute helicopter ride away. When our blood supply ran low, we would send for additional supply. There was one particular night when a bunch of Afghans in our partner force were gravely injured and we took them to our facility for treatment, which included giving some of them blood to stay alive. Suddenly, I saw a report that the weather forecast was changing, and there would soon be harsh conditions in the area. I knew that helicopters wouldn't be able to fly, and realized that we wouldn't be able to get additional blood anytime soon.

I asked the medics in our unit how much blood we had left, and they told me we were down to four units, and that one of the injured Afghans was requiring more blood—that, in fact, he might die without it. Normally, they would have just used the blood—it was only because I thought to ask, given the bad weather forecast, that this even became an issue. Under the military's guidelines, Americans have to get first priority for medical treatment—we were privileged to be able to treat the Afghans and help them when we could, but our highest duty is to preserve and save American lives. So I made the hard choice to tell our medics not to use the remaining blood until the weather cleared and we could be resupplied. I felt it was my duty to keep some blood in reserve in case Americans needed it before we could replenish the supply. In a perfect world, there would have been enough time to know for sure—whether there would be injured Americans, whether the Afghan would die, how long it would be until the weather cleared. But that information wasn't going to exist until it was too late to make the decision, and so I had to use my intuition and make the hard call without any definitive answers to rely on.

Twenty minutes later, I got word that there had been an incident on the battlefield, and two severely injured Americans were heading our way, desperately in need of blood. My decision to conserve the blood unquestionably saved American lives. The medics asked me afterward how my first thought had been to check on blood supply when I heard about the weather conditions, and my best answer was that I had an instinct. I was used to answering a particular question, a key one in hard situations: "What are we missing here?" I was always thinking about contingencies and making the associated hard decisions. I knew, in this case, there was no useful information I could gather, and no time to wait. Fortunately, the Afghan ended up surviving as well, and the decision I made avoided an unfortunate tragedy.

+ + +

In this instance, there might have been no turning back if it had turned out the Afghan's condition became more critical and we still weren't able to get more blood from Kandahar, but it's often the case that not every decision has to be the last decision. We forget sometimes that the right decision for now doesn't need to be locked in as the decision forever. If circumstances change or new knowledge appears, we can make a better decision as we move forward. We need to be agile in everything we do, constantly reevaluating, making sure that the course that was right ten minutes ago is still the right course. It's the lesson of sunk costs, which ends up applying in every sector—military, government, business, and our personal lives. You can't let ego stand in your way, or the reluctance to admit a mistake, or the unwillingness to acknowledge that something is happening that you didn't foresee. Dropping a bomb is a decision I couldn't take back—and so I had to be as sure I was right as anyone in my situation could possibly be. But many decisions are not quite so final. We can change roles, move headquarters, add features, cut prices, or shift priorities. A big part of deciding when to make a decision is thinking about what options are truly closed once that decision is made and what options merely get a bit more challenging. That kind of thinking always has to be part of the calculation.

Bring Your Values to Bear in Every Decision You Make

Finally, when I talk about learning how to think, part of what that means is not merely following a set of predetermined rules. The biggest problem with predetermined rules is that they can stop you from thinking about the bigger picture and making sure that what you're doing makes sense, makes you proud, and isn't something you're going to regret down the road.

In the military, we talk about acceptable casualties. It's a reality of war—there are situations where civilians do pay the ultimate price, through no fault of their own. If you find out that Adolf Hitler or Osama bin Laden is in a house with one hundred innocent civilians, what do you do? Do you drop a bomb, or do you say no, you won't kill those hundred civilians, even if letting that particular person survive means that thousands and thousands more innocent civilians might end up dead a week later because of what you didn't do?

Like I've said, my team was extremely fortunate that we never harmed anyone we shouldn't have—but the killing of civilians is a real problem during wartime, for obvious reasons. It will turn the population against you. In Afghanistan and Iraq, we needed the locals on our side. We needed those villagers to work with us, not against us, both for our own protection and theirs. In Afghanistan, we needed them to tell us that they saw the Taliban put a bomb in that road over there, before we drove over it, instead of pointing us that way with smiles on their faces. We also needed them to let us help them, to train them to govern themselves, to build infrastructure, and to rebuild their society.

To ensure civilian casualties were as limited as possible, and that the innocent Afghan civilians wouldn't turn against our forces, the military set up a policy called Boots on the Ground Battle Damage Assessment (BOG-BDA). This meant that after every bomb we dropped, we were required to physically go to the site to confirm that no civilians had been killed. The theory—a smart theory—was that knowing we would have to acknowledge civilian casualties would make it less likely that there would be any civilian casualties.

A talented team of Army Green Berets within my command had intelligence at one point that there were approximately ten Taliban members gathered together at three in the morning, in an area no civilian would ever go, and certainly not at that time. The team used surveillance techniques to view the site, and we knew, as a certainty, that there were no civilians there. They asked me for permission to drop a bomb from an unmanned aircraft, and following the decision-making process I had put in place, I granted it. They went ahead, and eight of the Taliban fighters were killed. An Army Colonel from the Commanding General's staff in Afghanistan called and asked my watch officer for our BDA report, and my watch officer explained that we didn't have one—that it was simply too much risk for not a good enough reason. The road to the site was too dangerous to travel, we knew there were no civilians present, and to ask anyone on my team to go down this isolated path in the middle of the night was an unnecessary risk to their lives, and one it made no sense to take.

I got on the phone with the Colonel and we went back and forth.

"This is the policy."

"But the policy, in this case, makes no sense. To achieve an already-known outcome, I will not take unnecessary risk that my men will die."

There are consequences in the military to not following the orders of a superior. (Truth is, the lack of organizational flexibility is a huge problem for the military—on the ground, we were living a "Never Agile Enough" kind of life, but in terms of the larger hierarchy, the structure has its weaknesses.) I could have been fired and sent home from the deployment as insubordinate. But in that moment, I couldn't just blindly follow the policy. I had to act consistently with my values, and make a judgment and a subsequent decision that I was going to be able to live with if the worst happened.

The Colonel said that since I wouldn't comply, he was going to report my noncompliance to his boss, the Commanding General in Afghanistan, and that he would ask his peer in charge of our Afghan partner force to order his men to unilaterally inspect the site instead. I urged him not to do that, but that decision was out of my hands. Twelve Afghan soldiers drove down that isolated road in three vehicles to make their assessment of the bomb site. The first two trucks hit an IED and three of the eight people in those two vehicles were killed, with others seriously wounded.

Soon after, I flew by helicopter to the outstation where the Green Beret team was stationed, sat with them, and told them how incredibly proud I was of their amazing bravery, the remarkable work they did night after dangerous night. It was one of the more emotional moments of my life. As we started our meeting, silence fell over the room, and one of the guys on the team opened by looking me square in the eyes and quietly but resolutely thanking me. He knew that the easier decision would have been caving to the pressure from above and deviating from my beliefs—and we all knew that would have meant some of the men in that room would have died.

The Green Beret had no idea that his words made my throat almost close as I choked up, and how hard I had to fight off tears. I was simply overwhelmed by the real-life impact, by the reality of the situation. The overwhelming magnitude of these kinds of decisions, made under the pressures of intense, nightly combat, take a toll on people that is difficult to understand for those who haven't experienced it. Now, with the benefit of several years of hindsight and the time to fully reflect on those past events, I have an even greater belief in the importance of process—your own process—and of values-based decision-making. Process can, no exaggeration, save people's lives.

+ + +

Most of the decisions we make aren't life-or-death. But we still need a smart process, and to follow our instincts and trust our values above all else. You need to be able to defend the choices you make, stand behind them, and go to sleep at night without regrets. You also need to realize that sometimes, it's not about making the right decision yourself, but, as I said in chapter 4, about ensuring the best decision gets made—by someone.

The next chapter is about creating organizations where the best decisions can and do get made, and about being the kind of leader who empowers everyone to be their best. Success is about more than just your own decision-making process—it's about having an organizational culture that brings out the strongest contributions from everyone, so that whether it's you making a decision or someone in a completely different role, in a completely different location, facing a completely new circumstance, that decision is the right one, and everyone feels heard, understood, and respected.

CHAPTER 6

GAIN AUTHORITY BY GIVING IT AWAY

Agility in the Organizations You Lead

I wrote in chapter 4 about Mark and his brave team based in Tarin Kowt, Afghanistan, birthplace of Mullah Omar, the Taliban's founder. Mark's team, with little warning or time to prepare, helicoptered into the middle of a gunfight to help another platoon beat back an assault by Taliban fighters. Their work was inspiring—but not everything went according to plan that night. With Mark's team on that mission was a committed, passionate SEAL named Shawn—who should have been at headquarters, not on a battlefield miles away.

The explanation of how Shawn got into the helicopter that night starts with a bit of a primer on the roles people fill on deployment. Shawn was an enlisted SEAL serving as my watch officer at the time, a critical role I mentioned earlier that involves being a bridge between the SEALs out in the field and the doctors, intelligence officers, pilots, technology experts, and support personnel in the tactical operations center back at HQ. You need a watch officer who knows and understands the battlefield and can provide necessary perspective to people filling all the other functions on the team, helping to coordinate what they need to do and when they need to do it, in order to best serve the team and ensure mission success.

That said, it's not the most exciting role for someone who's motivated by the adrenaline rush of being in the field. Shawn was in the role not as a reward for his tactical expertise, but as a punishment. While he was undeniably skilled, motivated, and well-intentioned, Shawn had also been involved in a situation at one of the outstations in which he became a distraction instead of a productive member of his team. I decided to move Shawn to the watch officer role, where I knew he could excel, where he would learn and grow, and where I would be able to keep a closer eye on him.

At any given time, there were two watch officers on duty—an enlisted SEAL like Shawn, and a SEAL officer (a future platoon leader). It was imperative that someone be in that role at all times, but most particularly at a time when Mark's platoon—a quick-reaction force co-located at headquarters with me, ready to deploy anywhere they were needed in the field in case of emergency—was needed.

Over the ten-month deployment, Mark's platoon was always ready to reinforce another platoon in the midst of battle, but the number of times we actually needed them to drop their own mission and head out the door at a moment's notice was fewer than ten. Sending them in was a big decision that carried significant coordination and execution risk, not to mention the opportunity cost of whatever they were supposed to be doing—and it was a decision that put a significant amount of responsibility on a watch officer like Shawn.

Whenever two people or units are trying to link up in the middle of the night, it inevitably proves to be more difficult than it sounds. SEALs are always pursuing ever-improving technology to mitigate risks, but ironically, one of the riskier things to do in the middle of the night is to simply link up: How does each unit know that the approaching troops are friendly? Imagine being fully loaded and out for combat in the dark of night, with a known enemy hunting you. No matter how well you coordinate with your "friends," there's a moment when the two units are close to each other but haven't yet confirmed who's who. The two friendly forces don't want to say anything out loud or use visible light signals—or they risk giving themselves away to the actual enemy. So as you see the other unit approaching, how do you positively identify that it's your friend and not an enemy? If you mistakenly assume it's your friend, you can be mortally surprised. If you mistakenly assume it's an enemy, the consequences can be equally fatal.

The situation only gets more complex when you add helicopters, jets, unmanned aircrafts, mortars, rockets, and other long-distance weapons systems into the mix. These are the moments a watch officer—coordinating all the elements out in the field, managing the back-and-forth communication, seeing the signs of danger ahead, and warning the troops on the ground—is of the highest importance.

And yet Shawn wasn't there. He knew Mark's team was being sent out on this critical mission—and look, I get it, this was the kind of mission Shawn lived for, the kind of mission that was the reason every SEAL wants to be a SEAL. I had pulled him away from the action for two months to sit in headquarters as a watch officer—an eternity on a ten-month deployment—and he was frustrated. He wanted to be out there, doing the job he had signed up to do. And so Shawn walked to the corner of the compound, talked to the senior enlisted SEAL who was organizing the mission, and told him that he had permission to go—when, in fact, he did not. He lied to get himself on the helicopter, and then, when we needed him in his position at headquarters, he wasn't there.

Fortunately, tragedy was avoided. Other people stepped up and covered Shawn's post, and the mission was a total success. We accomplished this without as much as a scratch on any of the SEALs, and Shawn's absence didn't lead to any negative consequences—except that it absolutely could have, and it was a selfish, shortsighted decision on his part. You simply don't leave your post without authorization, ever. You don't lie to your teammates. You don't make yourself a burden to the organization, not if you can help it. "Discipline is the soul of an army," George Washington once wrote. "It makes small numbers formidable; procures success to the weak, and esteem to all." It's one of my favorite quotes, and especially resonates given the small size of a SEAL Team compared to the larger military. Self-discipline is so critical as a member of an organization. Team, then teammate, then self—I can't reiterate it enough.

There were lots of things that I could have done in response to Shawn's actions. I could have permanently reduced his rank. I could have kicked him off my team and sent him home. I could have reduced his pay by 50 percent for six months. I could have held a "Trident Review Board" procedure and effectively removed

Shawn from the SEALs. Despite this very serious infraction—coming on top of the situation that had led me to put him in the watch officer position in the first place—I saw something in Shawn. I saw a good man, a deeply patriotic American who had talents and raw abilities that few possess.

I could have talked to Shawn behind closed doors, yelled at him, and made the situation about the two of us, about him disobeying a rule and me enforcing order and compliance. But it wasn't about the two of us. And it wasn't just about the rules, because there are always going to be times to break the rules (I'll talk about that more later in this chapter). This wasn't one of those times, and Shawn knew that. This was about finding the best way to make a SEAL realize his mistake and do better in the future—and, at the same time, about finding a way to extract whatever good I possibly could from a bad situation.

What I decided to do was hold a "Captain's mast," a nonjudicial proceeding in the Navy in which a Commanding Officer is authorized to conduct an inquiry into the facts surrounding a situation and impose punishment. And I brought two other officers, Josh and Rocky, into the process. They were eventually going to be in my role, commanding teams of their own, and I wanted to show them firsthand how to conduct a fair, proper disciplinary procedure. I wanted to demonstrate to them how you can use discipline without aiming to punish but instead hoping to help, to pull someone up instead of pushing them down.

Normally, a Captain's mast is very formal—in uniform, at attention, with rigid military customs being followed. I started the session off that way, but quickly pivoted to having us all simply sit at a table and talk. I asked Shawn what he thought the consequences of his actions could have been, and what might have happened back at headquarters to make that empty watch officer position critically important in the moment. And then I waited for him to reflect. I wanted him to go first, and actually think about what he had done. I had my answers, but I needed him to get there on his own—and then I could fill in the things he missed. Just telling someone the answer is never going to lead to as much learning and growth as if they can make the connections themselves.

We talked about how without him there, jets armed with bombs could have arrived late, doctors might not have been scrubbed in and ready for a casualty coming in, a medevac helicopter could have taken off late to pick up injured SEALs, or a situation could have unfolded at another outstation and there might have been no one at our watch officer's station to take their call and get them whatever help they needed. Being one minute or even one second late on any of these fronts can literally be the difference between life and death for SEALs on the battlefield. Having an additional SEAL on his mission was going to help Mark, absolutely—but the potential cost of Shawn missing from his post was much greater. At times we had more than five outstations in contact with enemy troops all at once. We regularly needed all hands on deck to manage many highly complicated situations. Not having Shawn available left us open to disaster.

Shawn, in making his decision to leave his post, was merely looking at the probability of his being needed at headquarters—which was low. But it's not just about probability. It's about the expected value of the outcome: probability multiplied by potential impact. The low probability of an incident where he'd be needed coupled with the huge impact if it had happened beats the higher probability of Shawn being marginally useful as just one more out of many in the field. Shawn's calculations were wrong—and even if they'd been right, you still don't abandon your post, because the effect of an empty position can be catastrophic.

After working our way through all this calmly and reasonably, we talked about Shawn's conflicting desires. He wanted to help, absolutely. But you can't lie to a teammate in order to get put on a mission, and you can't leave your post without permission, not even if you personally think it's the right thing to do at the time. I walked Shawn through my options, through the set of possible punishments I could impose on him. He knew that I had the authority to remove him from my SEAL Team, without question. He also knew that I was giving him a chance to take responsibility and commit to doing better.

I asked him to put himself in my shoes. If he were the Commanding Officer, looking holistically at the situation, what would he do? I always go into a proceeding like this with an idea about what the range of outcomes ought to be, and with a specific outcome in mind—but I am entirely open to learning new facts or hearing unexpected contrition that moves me in one direction or the other. Here I had heard what I hoped and expected to hear, and knew the punishment I'd be most comfortable issuing—but I also wanted Shawn to talk first and get there on his own, because it would make the punishment much more meaningful if it was one that he had essentially chosen for himself.

Shawn explained that he understood this wasn't just a small mistake to be brushed off. Merely having a Captain's mast while overseas demonstrated that this was serious. Shawn suggested, as I hoped and expected he would, that I reduce his rank for six months and that we could then reevaluate his performance at the end of the deployment. Together, we agreed that this would be his punishment, and we would move on from there. He would be a better teammate and a better SEAL going forward.

Shawn wrote me an email about two years after that deployment thanking me for how I had approached the situation and letting me know it had made him a better SEAL. Tragically, just a few weeks after sending me that note, Shawn died in a training accident and we lost an incredible American.

The lesson I learned from the situation—and the lesson I was hoping Josh and Rocky would also learn—was that you always need to think about the outcome you're trying to achieve with your actions, and the best future state that could emerge from a difficult situation. Walking through the process with me, Josh and Rocky saw how a leader can create the conditions for better long-term outcomes and keep emotions in check during a disciplinary hearing. They saw how to make the process work for the situation, and how to lift people up even as you impose necessary consequences for behavior.

Seeing the situation from the inside helped Josh and Rocky become better officers and leaders, just as it helped Shawn become a better SEAL. Collectively, Josh and Rocky had over twenty-five years of experience in the SEALs, but they told me they had never before seen a disciplinary proceeding work like that in the SEAL Teams—calm, reasonable, framed as a discussion and a learning opportunity for everyone, and where the person being punished actually chose the consequence for himself.

This, I felt—and still feel to this day—was a strong demonstration of what it means to lead an organization. You don't just act on your own behalf, exerting authority simply because you're entitled to and doling out the punishment that will satisfy you the most and make you look as strong as you can. Leaders often worry about coming off as weak—to their subordinates and to their superiors—and overcompensate by getting angry and taking their emotions out on others. But looking good, or feeling good, aren't the things a strong leader should be prioritizing. Instead, you have to focus on the needs of the entire organization, thinking about who you can teach in the process, what you can teach them, and how you can plant the seeds for behaviors that you would most want to see in the future. If someone is going to stay on the team, you make them better. If they need to leave, you let them leave with dignity and, in doing so, make them an ally in the future. Throughout the situation, you train the next generation at the same time as you execute your own duties. You set the tone that you want the entire organization to embody.

That last point is critical. The tone of an organization starts with the leader. The tone of any team, of any size, starts with the leader—so if you are the leader, you need to be especially conscious of what tone you set. I ran into one of my former SEALs, Rob, a few years later, after I'd joined the corporate world. He told me that the most lasting memory he had of me was when I had just taken over SEAL Team TWO and decided to fly out to Coronado, California, for his class's SEAL graduation—not because I had to, but because I wanted to be there and welcome the ten new SEALs from that class who would join my SEAL Team in just a few weeks.

My goal was to make it clear that people new to the SEAL Team were valued tremendously, integral to our future success, and not just incidental additions. These newcomers would bring fresh perspective, untethered from the notion that we do things a certain way because we've always done them that way. I would be counting on them to step up and contribute—to be leaders when needed—and I wanted them to know that. Rob still remembered the speech I gave, and said it was so meaningful that as a leader, I thought it was worth coming to graduation, just to welcome the new guys. My intent had clearly made an impact.

Hearing Rob say all that more than five years after it happened validated so many decisions I had made along the way, thinking about the most junior people on the team even while being in charge. Every leader must, at all times, keep as many people on their team in mind as possible. And the thing is, everyone who isn't a leader has to do that, too. Just like I've already said, we all have to be ready to be the leader at any given time. That's how we make sure our organization is agile enough to succeed. We all have to be ready to move forward and move back as needed. So any advice about leadership is not just for the ones with the elevated titles—the CEOs, the vice presidents, the directors—it's for everybody who might ever need to make a decision, steer the ship, or work alongside others. It's for everybody on any team or in any organization, because we are all leaders in some way, at some time. In that spirit, there are four leadership principles that I think about every day, and that I want to spend the rest of this chapter discussing.

Use Your Ability and Capacity to Pull Others Up

This was what I was trying to do with Shawn—and with Josh and Rocky. I was thinking not just about Shawn, but also about how to use the situation to help Josh and Rocky be better. To do this effectively means first connecting the organization's mission to the needs and goals of everyone on the team. It means reading people—like Ray Dalio at Bridgewater was able to read me—and understanding what motivates them, what drives them to wake up in the morning. In many ways, great team players at any level are simply great listeners who can connect the dots that are out there waiting to be connected.

With Shawn, I didn't just say, "You did X, so now Y is going to happen to you." I tried to put him in my shoes, to help him see the problem and all the considerations around it. I tried to help him see how I needed to make my decision, what the process was, and what factors I needed to consider. And then, I had to flip it around and put myself in his shoes, in order to effectively understand what he needed from me in that moment, to comprehend what he'd done wrong and how he could do better. What defines an organization isn't whether people fail—people will always fail—but how the organization handles those bad actions, and whether they can use them as springboards to make the future better.

In disciplining Shawn, or anyone else over the course of my career, I needed to remember that while everyone is motivated by different things, at an elemental level people are driven by mostly the same things: family, quality of life, teaching, learning, getting promoted, receiving public recognition, compensation, connection to a mission, faith, being part of a team, and maybe a handful more. Good leaders recognize that people are wired differently, and withhold judgment when dealing with people who are motivated by something other than what motivates the leader. I may not be driven by having the largest bank account or by receiving public recognition, but that doesn't mean I can't accept that for others those might be their primary goals, and it doesn't mean I can't do my best to help them achieve those goals through our work together. At the same time, we have to use our knowledge of people's motivations in a purposeful, deliberate way.

We are biased, as I said in the last chapter, to like people who are like us. But as leaders we have to connect with everyone, not just those who think the same way we do. Helping people see how achieving the organizational goals can also satisfy their own individual motivations is one of the primary arts of leadership.

+ + +

The reality is that at the same time a good leader has to connect the larger mission with everyone's personal goals, that same leader also has to strive to lift everyone's personal goals to a higher level as well. Many people have great but shallow motivations for the work they do. They want more money, or a nicer house, or the adulation they believe will come with fame or notoriety. The best leaders know that what's most important is meaning. We'll get much more into meaning in the final section of the book, but for now, I want to make the point that leaders do best when they can influence their team to make a bigger impact on the people they serve, and on the world. Leaders help people find their bigger and deeper reasons for why they do what they do. They help people identify the impacts they want to make, and then help them make them. They align passions to larger causes. They help their people know, and then they help their people act, organizing them in the way that best achieves the strategy of the larger organization.

Part of this means knowing yourself and your own goals and motivations when it comes to the roles you want to play in an organization. As a White House Fellow, I ended up with fourteen

interviews in a week to figure out which job I would fill—at the
Department of Agriculture, the Small Business Administration,
the Department of Commerce, and more—forcing me to think
about what I really wanted from the program. Did I want to go
deeper in an area I already knew something about (national security and foreign policy), or did I want to explore something new
and add to my diversity of expertise? Breadth versus depth was
the trade-off I found myself thinking about as I went through
the process, and just like when I made the decision to become a
SEAL rather than a pilot, I needed to better understand myself
before I could make the right choice.

When I sat in the room interviewing for the role I ultimately
took, I was interviewing the interviewer just as much as he was
interviewing me. I had to make sure the role was the right one,
a position that would allow me to use my skills and create the
most impact—not just now, but over a long career. I had pur-
sued the White House Fellows program as part of my general
orientation toward tackling the hardest challenges in life—and
I needed to keep that mission in mind.

Again, it's the "how to think, not what to think" lesson. Even
in a setting when there seems to be only one answer—do you
really say no to the Deputy National Security Advisor if it turns
out that he offers you the job?—you have to ask yourself the
right questions to make sure you're making the best decision.

As the interview went on, I realized the position I was being
offered was a substantial one, a position of responsibility for defense strategy, overseeing an interagency policymaking process,
and an opportunity to work directly in the White House, running meetings in the Situation Room. As we talked, I knew the

way to make the most impact was going to be to go deeper into the world of national security and not simply grow my breadth of knowledge. But it was absolutely a trade-off, and, for someone else, another decision may have been just as correct. It simply depended on personal goals and preferences.

+ + +

There's another way we must all use our capacities to pull the rest of our team up. We have to keep our attitude in mind. An infectiously positive attitude is a force multiplier—it gives us the ability to perform greater feats than we would be able to without it. Further, we can help our team members by being what I call a "stress sponge." We have a choice at any moment to either create stress or absorb it. Whenever I can absorb someone else's stress—solve their problem, let them off the hook, remove an obstacle in their way—I do it, not only because it helps them individually but because it helps the entire team. This doesn't mean they can stop striving to do everything they can—but it means they know that the leader has their back. These are the actions leaders can take to make themselves into the kinds of people about whom others say, "I'd follow him anywhere."

There are so many people I've worked with over the years who I'd follow anywhere because I trust that no matter what situation we find ourselves in, they have my back, they're looking out for me, and they're working to make things better, not worse. They're the people constantly focused on using their abilities and capacities to pull people up, and it's what makes them great leaders.

Give Yourself Space to Think About What Not to Do

In the last chapter, when I talked about realizing we needed to conserve blood in the blood bank as bad weather rolled in, one of the reasons I was able to think about issues like that—future considerations, rather than the immediate concerns of the moment—is that I made sure as a leader that I had space to think about what not to do, space to keep my eye on bigger-picture issues, space to reflect and plan . . . and lead. After all, you can't think about the white space when you're in the weeds of a problem.

I've never met any senior person in any organization who has told me that they need more work to do, or that they're bored. Competent people in any organization are inevitably given more to do than they can handle, because there are things that need to get done, and it's easy to go to the person who can handle it. (When you want something done, the old saying goes, ask a busy person.) At the same time, it can be very tempting—whether you're running an organization or aspiring to move up the ranks—to think that you are the only person who can or should be doing a particular task. That's exactly the opposite of the right way to think. When I walk into any organization to give a talk, I often ask, "Who here is in charge of what your organization isn't doing?" Being able to see the negative space—to know where the gaps are, what tasks are unnecessary, who is wasting their time—is critical to finding opportunities and seeing risks.

No one ever raises a hand, because we don't allocate work that way. No one is given the job of taking work off people's plates, of moving it either down the chain—to someone who can be challenged by it, learn from it, and embrace a new opportunity—or moving it off the list of tasks completely, because it doesn't actually need to get done. Leadership in this area involves pushing as much work down to lower levels as possible. This creates awesome opportunities for more junior employees, and it also creates space for higher-level staff to think strategically instead of being wall-to-wall packed with urgent tasks that must get done.

Put simply, you want to use your comparative advantage, and find the comparative advantages of everyone around you. Don't get sucked into doing things that others can do just as well (or even better) than you can, and design your organization so that work lands in the right spot. A good organization celebrates delegation.

It's such a critical point. Just like I gave Reed the opportunity to become my go-to expert in solving the power problem, we can all help others gain new skills—or use the chance to delegate as a way to learn where someone's capacity ends. If you assign a desired outcome to someone else, you will see if they can do it or not. If they do it, you just achieved something without spending any of your own time on it. If they don't do it, perhaps they've learned enough to do it next time, or perhaps you've learned that you've maxed out someone's capability, at least for right now.

And sure, you don't put the second string in when it's an urgent, must-win situation. When there's no margin for error, you have to go with the A team. But when we can think about the long run, when the risk tolerance allows it, you take a second-stringer and put them in the lead. You train your bench. They will learn and get better, or everyone will realize their limits. No one wakes up and asks what they can screw up today. We have to hold people to a high standard at every turn, but we also have to give them opportunities to learn if we ever expect them to succeed and move from the B team to the A team.

That brings up a larger point I mentioned earlier: individuals can fail, but organizations can't. As leaders, we should be pushing people to the point of (safe and sensible) failure, because that's how they will learn and improve—but we need to do so while at the same time understanding what level of failure the organization can tolerate and still achieve its mission. When it's okay to make a mistake, you put in the team that might still need more training. When everything is on the line, you need to realize that you may not have the luxury to do that.

At an organizational level, having everyone understand that they will be pushed to their limits—and that the leader isn't going to do everything himself—sets up a situation where success is reliant on everyone, not just the person at the top. It also sets up a dynamic where people know that they will be trusted with as much as they can handle, and it gives them confidence that their skills and talents will be recognized.

✦ ✦ ✦

Delegating isn't just for discrete tasks. It's also about decision-making authority. We don't need to assert the greatest amount of authority that we're entitled to. Our organizations are better served by training the people below us to one day take our place. The more we can pass down the chain of command, the better equipped our organization will be, with more capable leaders throughout. True leadership is realizing, as I've said before, that you don't need to make the best decision, you just need to ensure the best decision gets made. Similarly, you don't need to play every instrument. As the leader, you simply conduct the band.

By moving out of people's way and letting them shine, we not only tell them that they are critical to the team's success—we show them. We want to make sure that everyone from the lowest level to the highest feels like they're important and given as much responsibility as they can handle. When touring NASA in 1962, President Kennedy asked a janitor what his job involved, and he told the President that he was helping to put a man on the moon. That was the perfect answer, and it's the kind of answer we should want everyone in our organization to feel empowered to give. No one on my team works "for" me. We all work with each other, for each other, and for the team. We are all vital to mission success.

+ + +

Right alongside the idea of delegating should be the goal of exposing everyone in the organization to as much as they're able to see. This accomplishes a few things. First, it allows people to feel as invested as possible in the organization's big-picture mission. Second, it helps them to more fully appreciate the roles that others play in achieving success. Third, it lets them potentially discover new areas of interest or talent where they can make a contribution, either now or in the future.

There were nights in my team's deployment to Afghanistan when things were quiet. I saw two of my younger SEALs, Bo and Chris, at dinner one night after they hadn't gone out for two nights in a row. I asked what they were planning on doing, and they said they would probably just relax, maybe play a little

Xbox. I told them that there were seven Afghans in the medical unit, from a mass casualty situation where we were helping to treat some of the injured men, and that our medical staff could use some extra hands. I asked if they would be up for spending several hours that night helping out—and improving their "battlefield trauma" skills, in case they ever need them.

The question of Xbox versus more experience was an easy one for them—you can't miss an opportunity to make yourself better. Every SEAL has an obligation to his teammates to be able to calmly and competently respond to a teammate being shot or blown up. And even though I couldn't have imagined how it would end up playing out down the line (as you'll soon see), it proved to me the lesson that doing the smart thing pays off, even if in the moment you don't quite know how it will.

In the medical facility, we had three doctors and a staff of about thirty-five healthcare professionals. When we had capacity or it was strategic to the mission, we would do whatever we could to treat members of our Afghan partner forces or injured civilians. Our professionals were often maxed out, and Bo and Chris were tremendously helpful that night.

The next morning, the two of them thanked me for pushing them to help. They said the extreme situations and traumas they witnessed and assisted with were enlightening for them, and incredibly helpful as they moved forward in the deployment, especially watching how brilliantly competent the doctors and staff were and how much good they were doing for the injured Afghans. I didn't think anything of it—I tried to expose the younger SEALs to as many facets of the organization as I could—until a few weeks later, when I got a call in the operations center: "Two Sierra Whiskey"—code for two SEALs wounded on a mission. That kind of call doesn't come through unless injuries are serious and medical attention will be needed. We don't share names over the radio, so until their roster numbers were transmitted, I was left to wonder and worry about which of my men were hurt—and once I knew, I was hoping for the best as our dedicated medevac helicopter flew the 6 to 8 minutes to retrieve them from the field. While they were flying back, I got word that the troops-in-combat (TIC) call was over, and the gunfight had ended—which freed me to go to the landing zone and meet the helicopter as it arrived.

I saw Bo and Chris on the helicopter, critically wounded. An explosion had severed one of Bo's legs and badly damaged the other, and had blown up right in Chris's face, making his eyes and much of his facial structure nearly unrecognizable. Bo had three tourniquets on his leg, one of which had come off—so I ended up holding pressure on heavy arterial bleeding from his knee. The two of them were in incredible pain, even with the painkillers—fentanyl "lollipops"—they had been given on the helicopter. I tried to calmly ease any back-of-the-mind worries they might have had—I told them that I had confidence they were both going to be fine, that I would personally call their families to let them know what had happened, that they were about to receive incredible care, and that they would be the ones calling their families themselves as soon as they were treated.

The medic in the field, incidentally, showed extreme bravery in the situation. Bo and Chris were numbers two and three in the patrol that day. Somehow, the point man at the front had stepped over the bomb and escaped without a scratch. Our medic, nicknamed Nunchuck, was number six . . . and he had to navigate a literal minefield to treat Bo and Chris, hoping that there weren't more unexploded bombs in the area. He went right up to them, without an ounce of fear, and began to use his incredible medical training and instincts to help them.

Both Bo and Chris survived, albeit with serious injuries that will impact the rest of their lives. But what sticks with me is that weeks later, they thanked me—they said, "Mr. Hayes, we felt comfort because we knew where we were and what was going to happen. We knew the quality of the doctors and the organization of the system, because of the night you had us train in the medical unit."

It really did make a difference for them, and paid dividends—though of course not in the way anyone would have expected. Chris eventually regained partial sight in one eye, but wasn't able to stay in the SEALs. Instead, he discovered a new passion, and decided his life's calling was to help others as a physician. As of this writing, he is now a doctor doing his medical residency. Chris's story hammers home the importance of exposing people to every facet of an organization, because you never know what someone's true mission might be, and what hidden passions you might unlock in them.

Share Credit, Share Blame

The high-performing team succeeds or fails together. The best leaders don't need credit, and aren't afraid to accept blame. Both halves of that sentence can be harder than they seem. Lots of people see the state of the world as a zero-sum game. They see a limited amount of credit to go around, and a fixed amount of blame. If someone else is getting credit, they don't think there's any credit left for them to enjoy. And if they're being blamed, they imagine it means everyone else is getting off scot-free. This is an attitude that just doesn't work in a well-functioning, high-performing team situation. Real leaders know that any one person's success is their success. Real leaders are happy when they're able to step aside and put others in a position to receive credit. Real leaders just need their people and their organization to win.

Imagine a SEAL operation that goes incredibly well. These missions, by definition, require great risk and precision, and have zero room for error. They often have one or a few people who did the very last tactical action that yielded success. Recall the situation in chapter 4 where I captured the second-most-wanted terrorist. Yes, I performed that tactical action—but it was our entire team working together that created that success, and my last action could and would have been done by any SEAL on that mission. And not just the SEALs themselves. There are a great number of non-SEALs who also enable our missions to succeed. Intelligence specialists, communications experts, and the procurement professionals who buy the clothes on the SEALs' backs, just as a few examples. They all contribute to the mission. There are always adjacent units who supplied and flew the helicopters, jets, and unmanned aerial vehicles. And there are people in the Pentagon or at the local embassy who gave permission for an operation to occur.

It can be very easy to be a SEAL after one of these missions and not think about the entire universe of people who enabled success. We aspire to spread credit for that success to everyone beyond the SEAL Team by identifying them, sharing with them what we can about the operation, helping them see their role in reaching the goal, and saying thank you. Good leaders help their organization to systematically spread credit and say thanks.

We can also, of course, think about the inverse, about the operation that goes terribly wrong. Maybe the goal isn't reached, or maybe there is unintended death or permanent injury, causing great emotional trauma and affecting people and families well beyond the SEAL Team. The ingredients to break down a high-performing team are all present in these situations. Emotions like anger and sadness can destroy a team and limit future success. Leaders, even if they can't see what they personally did wrong, are still responsible for the outcome. Everyone needs to share blame equally as a team and ensure no one person takes more—or less—than necessary. That's how the team stays together, focused, and agile enough to win the next time.

+ + +

To live these values requires a certain level of security. If you're afraid of someone else getting credit, it changes who you want to have around you. People who are insecure in their role don't want to work with people better than themselves, don't want to delegate tasks to others who might actually do them well, and aren't putting the needs of the team first. In the best situations, as a leader, you want to be able to work yourself out of a job. You want to work with people who are so good that they make you unnecessary. You want to hire them, build a culture where everyone knows they can step up as needed, and then get out of people's way.

It can take some time to get comfortable with that kind of thinking. In my mind, there are three phases of a career. In the first phase, you're trying to learn a set of skills as well as you can, building a foundation, and becoming an expert. In the second phase, you're trying to show the world what you can do and prove that you are good, establish dominance, and get recognized as an expert. But in the third phase, you have nothing left to prove. You are secure in your capabilities and comfortable with your status, and that's when you can unlock the most potential. That's when you live to enable the success of others, when you trust the people around you, and you realize that the greatest recognition a leader can get is from building a team that everyone knows is great. You're liberated at that point. You understand that mistakes might happen, and you no longer fear them. They're learning opportunities—for you, and for everyone that surrounds you. One of the greatest measures of a leader is to look at how many other leaders they have created.

The only reasons not to hire someone better than you center around discomfort and fear. But if you own the outcomes of your team—if you recognize that credit is shared all around—you have nothing to worry about. Team success is your success. Individual success is your success. In that third phase, you become a mentor and a teacher. You become able to finally see not just what motivates you but what motivates everyone around you—and you can dedicate yourself to helping others achieve their goals.

Foster a "Run and Renovate" Culture

The strongest leaders ask everyone in their organization to think on two levels: run, and renovate. What I mean by that is that we need everyone to think short-term and long-term at the same time. You need to get the job done in the moment ("run") but you also need to figure out what ought to change to enable the greatest amount of long-term success ("renovate"). At every level, the best contributors keep both of these levels in mind in all that they do. You can run the system you're in, but at the same time work to fix the system and change the rules of the game.

By nature, SEALs are rule breakers—like Shawn. They're the kind of people who think they know best, and only want to follow rules that they agree with. This isn't a bad thing if it's harnessed properly. We want people to be aggressive and make things happen. We don't want people to follow rules if the rules are wrong and get in the way of mission success. But we also need people with impeccable judgment, to know when it's okay to bend or break a rule, and when doing so will have unintended consequences that ultimately hurt the team.

When I think about agility, a big part is about rule following and rule breaking, and when to do which. Organizations make leaps when people recognize that some expectations are wrong, and there are better ways to do things. We need to follow rules, of course. But we also need to be laser-focused on advocating for change when rules are wrong.

In a lot of ways, the run/renovate balance depends on your organization. You need to assess the ability to change, how fast things will be able to shift—and then you push right to the edge of that limit. The SEALs had been around for more than thirty years when I joined. I had to pick my battles, and tried to work with others to change the culture from "mission success at all costs" to thinking more strategically about the bigger picture. Then, by the time I was in a position of leadership, we were ready to focus on things like the reconciliation program I talked about in the introduction.

I have another example of how to bring change to an organization. In 2005, there was a mass casualty situation on Operation Red Wings in Afghanistan, where eight SEALs and eight aircrew died in a helicopter shoot-down as, outnumbered by Taliban forces, they attempted a bold daylight rescue mission to save four SEALs. (This situation was chronicled in the book and movie *Lone Survivor*.) I took over command for the surviving SEALs in the unit, replacing their task unit commander, who'd been shot down. There was unimaginable pain in the unit after what had happened, all kinds of natural feelings in the wake of not only losing friends and teammates, but being the ones who had to land and recover their bodies after such a catastrophic shoot-down. There's an ethos in the SEALs—really in the military as a whole—of suffering in silence, and at the time (and even today, to a lesser degree), people didn't understand the value of talking about their experiences and getting help when they could use it. My mom spent her career as a social worker and counselor, and having grown up with her excellent influence, I knew everyone on the team would benefit from talking to someone.

I facilitated a chaplain and a psychologist coming overseas to see the team, and told everyone that these were resources I wanted them to use, and that there should be no stigma in doing so. There was a wide range of opinions expressed among the team about whether this would be useful, or even acceptable—ranging from appreciation to outright refusal to consider the help. I gathered everyone together and told them that it was nonnegotiable. I'd had several private and forever-confidential conversations with guys in the room, and I knew that many of them were dealing with symptoms of traumatic stress (absolutely to be expected after an event like this) and would benefit from talking to a trained professional—so it was something that we as a team needed to make possible.

I told those who were not interested that they had to respect the fact that while they might not personally think this was useful help, we all needed to support our teammates. In that spirit, I required everyone on the team to see the chaplain and psychologist for at least five minutes. I said I didn't care whether they sat and said hello and nothing else for the five minutes. Everyone needed to do it so there would be no stigma either way. While the chaplain and the psychologist never violated any confidentiality, they kept me informed about how the group was doing—and they told me that every single person opened up and asked for a follow-up meeting. The strongest naysayers became the most enthusiastic consumers of the help. After a week, the chaplain and the psychologist each said they needed to extend their trip indefinitely. Many of the guys on the team privately told me that these counselors were a huge help, and they asked for more and more time with them. It ended up making such a difference in so many lives. There was such a clear need.

I used that experience to advocate for a full-time psychologist to be available to every SEAL Team—and I was successful in making that case. It wasn't easy. Aside from the stigma about mental health issues, there was also concern within the SEALs about becoming too support-heavy. To stay agile as a team, we need to be lean, and have only as much support as we absolutely require. I call it the "tooth-to-tail ratio." You need lots of teeth—and no more tail than necessary—or you're going to inevitably be slower to move and respond. Too many nonessential functions can easily drag an organization down and make it harder to keep focus on the mission. But this was something I felt so strongly about, and I knew it would prove worthwhile.

"Run and renovate" means more than just advocating for

change. It's a concept that should be top of mind in almost everything you do—as a leader or as someone looking to lead one day. It infuses even the smallest conversations. When you push a teammate—when you challenge something they've done or try to initiate a hard conversation—you need to be thinking about how you're trying to affect them in the moment ("run") and how you're trying to shape their future ("renovate"). It's the kind of thinking I did when I was deciding how to approach my Captain's mast with Shawn—how to best take care of the present situation, where he had left his post, but also how to shape him into a better SEAL moving forward. We have to know how to connect to people to make the change we need to see right now, but also create the best chance for the right behavior in the future.

This last story almost perfectly illustrates this point. I had the privilege of seeing another country's BUD/S-equivalent training class go through Hell Week. This was normally not open to outsiders, but this country had modeled their training program on ours, and we were there to work together and for them to show off and demonstrate what a rigorous program they had created. It was a much smaller force, known as Tactical Divers, and they are a world-class unit. Their class was down to three people at the point we saw them, and they were truly miserable, in ways we had not been in BUD/S.

Their instructor drove us on a beautiful ride through an incredible countryside to one final station, in the middle of nowhere, with temperatures in the low forties, howling winds, and light rain. Finally, we got to where we were heading, and the instructor stopped the car as we approached a steep cliff. I couldn't believe what I saw when I got out of the vehicle. There were three crucifixes set up, right on the edge of the cliff, each with a trainee tied to it about ten feet off the ground, held only by a rope. My immediate thought was, *What in the world is going on here?* The instructor started spraying them with water, whipping them, yelling at them, asking (in their native language), "Do you really want to be a SEAL?"

I couldn't unsee what I was seeing. This was too much. Training is supposed to be tough, but this was abuse, this was unacceptable. I wished I wasn't there, but I was—and from the looks on the faces of the two more junior SEALs from my platoon who had accompanied me, I could tell they were stunned as well. But what exactly was I supposed to do in that situation? If I was too aggressive in telling the instructors how to run their training program, I'd be seen as arrogant and preachy, and while they might change their actions in the moment, they would probably just ignore me in the long run and return to this same behavior. At the same time, I couldn't do nothing and just walk away.

I ran through the range of possibilities in my mind, thinking about the "run vs. renovate" idea. I wanted this to end now, but I also wanted to feel confident that they wouldn't put those men right back up on the crosses the moment we left. Knowing the culture, I didn't want to embarrass the instructor, and I didn't want to put him on the defensive. I could have yelled, made a big fuss, threatened to report them to . . . someone . . . and they would have surely taken the men down, but that wouldn't have gotten us to the ideal future state.

Instead, I pulled the senior guy aside and talked to him, one-on-one, in his language. I complimented him on how hard the training was, knowing he was trying to impress us. I told him that so much of it was even better than ours, and I was in awe. But I also said, gently, "I just have to share with you some thoughts about this current element and how we as American SEALs would push our students. This is honestly nothing that we would do," and I explained the difference, as I saw it, between humiliation and actual risk to someone's physical or mental well-being. I described how we find the line, and push our own students right to the edge of their breaking points but without doing any real harm.

I was ready to make the soft ask if I needed to, to ask if he would mind bringing them down from the crosses, and to tell him (with less incriminating language) that I couldn't be there while human rights abuses were going on. But he was one step ahead of me, and said, just as gently, "Okay, so we should just bring them down and start the next exercise, and we won't do that one again."

I had told him how I felt, not what to do, and I think that gave me the best chance of reaching the ideal outcome. I was focused on using the least amount of force necessary, so that for their next training class, they might think twice, and wouldn't feel like they had been pushed into the decision to change. I had simply given them input, and they made and owned their own decision—a decision more likely to endure for future classes.

Of course, if I thought those men had been in imminent danger, I would have used force to stop what was happening. But I kept my composure, going back to the lessons I outlined in the first section of the book about controlling emotions and being comfortable in uncomfortable situations. And I used the lessons in this chapter, about being a leader and enabling the best outcomes for the organization, in trying to push the instructor to see things in a different way. We went on, during the next exercise, to have a productive conversation about where to draw the line and how to find the limit of how hard to push, and I'm optimistic that I made a positive impact on their training program.

+ + +

Agility really is all about understanding situations and taking a flexible approach to reaching the desired outcome. That's the big principle behind these past three chapters. We need to be flexible in our roles, moving seamlessly between leading and following, and we need to be flexible in our decisions, setting up a framework that enables the most useful information to emerge and guide us even as situations change. Finally, we need to be flexible in how we structure our organizations, letting work land on the people who can do it best, training the next generation, sharing credit and blame, and always thinking about how to balance the short-term and the long-term, following and understanding the rules but at the same time knowing that sometimes we must advocate to change them.

In the final section of the book, we move from agility to meaning. Even the most excellent people in the most agile organization won't accomplish great things if they're not thinking about the meaning behind them. We need to connect with the people around us, with the driving purpose behind the work we do, and with the big picture of improving society and the world in order to live the most impactful lives we can. The final three chapters will cover these issues, and explain how we can create a world for ourselves that is full of meaning, satisfaction, and reward, while lifting up those around us.

SECTION III

NEVER MEANINGFUL ENOUGH

CHAPTER 7

PUSH YOUR VALUES OUT INTO THE WORLD

Finding Meaning as an Individual

There's more to the story I shared at the end of chapter 5, when I pushed back against the Army Colonel who insisted I send the Green Berets under my command down an explosive-laden road, putting them in needless danger, merely to follow protocol. When I first got off the phone with the Colonel, having made my decision but looking for guidance and comfort, I did something I so often did on the battlefield, but rarely talked about: I opened a travel-size Bible that a military chaplain had given me for my first overseas deployment, with a camouflaged cover emblazoned with the Navy SEAL Trident.

I kept this Bible with me at all times in service, because, for me, it provided comfort, solace, and support. My faith has been the core to who I am over my entire life, and it didn't stop when I went off to war. When I was young and struggling with a hard situation, my mom would flip the pages of her Bible, have me randomly stop my finger on a verse, and ask me to read. More often than not, I would find applicable wisdom or guidance in that random verse, and over time I grew to believe that "random" wasn't necessarily always so random. In my adulthood, I continued to flip the pages, hoping for help when I most needed it.

This time, my finger landed on a line, and with astonishment I read: "So if anyone tells you, 'There he is, out in the desert,' do not go out. . . . Wherever there is a carcass there the vultures will gather" (Matthew, 24:26–28).

The words applied directly to the dilemma at hand. The dead Taliban fighters were on the ground, and I was being asked to send my men out there, to the desert, to witness our work. As I wrote in chapter 5, I couldn't do it. It's absolutely the case that verses of scripture often find a way to apply to whatever the situation happens to be, but here the words were literally saying *Do not go out into the desert*. It couldn't have been clearer to me—the Bible was saying my decision had been the right one. And sure enough, sadly, a number of the Afghan men who were ordered to go into the desert by the Army Colonel did not survive.

When I was growing up, my grandfather would tell me how his faith had helped give him strength at Pearl Harbor, how it had compelled him to drive toward the water instead of racing in the other direction. I believe with every fiber of my being that he—and God—watched over me and guided my decisions in the field that night, as they've done for my entire life. That belief gave me strength so often in my service, and it gives me strength so often now.

But here's the thing: For me, it's faith; for you, it could be anything. It's not the specifics of my belief that matter in terms of helping me better my life and making me more effective in everything I do—it's the fact that I believe in *something*, that there's a core set of values driving my actions, an ethos I strive to live by, a North Star guiding me in the right direction, keeping me on the right track, or steering me when I fall short. We all fall short, inevitably, but what matters is how we handle those moments, and whether we can get back on course. There are men and women of all faiths—and of no organized faith at all—who have those kinds of values driving them, who lead exemplary lives of character and strength, who inspire those around them, and who take on missions that serve all of us.

If you have that kind of belief system in place, good for you. If not, it may take some hard work and introspection to figure out what truly motivates you, and what ultimately matters most. There are three parts, as I see them, to the journey to imbue your life with meaning, and that's what this chapter—and, really, this entire final section of the book—is about: first, we all have to believe in something; second, we have to identify and actually go out and do the things that are meaningful to us; and third, we have to realize that we can never predict the future, so we have to make decisions for now instead of waiting for a better time that may never come.

No Matter What You Believe In, Believe In Something

Where do you turn when you need help? Who gives you answers when you don't even understand the questions? What gives you the strength to put one foot in front of the other on the hardest days of your life?

Before I went off to lead SEAL Team TWO in Afghanistan, I had never before been responsible for the lives of so many individuals, in so many respects. There were about to be two thousand people under my command, each depending on me to make sure they came home safely—not to mention the family members waiting anxiously for their return. This hit home for me when I made an advance trip to visit the region I'd be commanding, as key leaders always do, to get the lay of the land and better understand the mission. Extensive predeployment training to figure out how to prepare with maximum efficiency to achieve the goals of the war and at the same time minimize risk is always a key part of SEAL command.

The feeling of responsibility for the lives of others isn't limited to the military, of course. Frank D'Souza is one of the exceedingly rare individuals who have founded a company and built it into a Fortune 200 enterprise. Before he stepped down as CEO of Cognizant after his twenty-fifth year of leadership, he and I talked about how much time he spent considering his role in the lives of the 280,000 people (and more than a million over time) he employed. We talked through a particular thought exercise I remember vividly: If a company merely covers its costs and creates shareholder value, is it worth it? Frank and I agreed that creating a firm that employs so many thousands of people and contributes in such a meaningful way to global productivity would be a wonderfully satisfying way to spend a life. Of course, Cognizant generates more than two billion dollars a year in free cash flow, so the exercise was merely theoretical. It did, however, emphasize to me the "people first" servant-leader orientation that is so important to hold in any organization.

While I was in Afghanistan on this predeployment trip, unfortunately there was an incident where a helicopter crashed and three SEALs died, while a fourth was very badly wounded. I went to the memorial service for those who died, and it was a horrible reminder of the very real risks of service, and of the profound responsibility I would soon have for my team.

For the first leg of my flight back home from Kandahar, my leadership team and I ended up on a medevac plane to Germany that had a handful of extra seats. There were fifteen medical professionals on the plane treating seven seriously wounded soldiers, and I found myself in a military jump seat next to an elevated gurney, carrying a man in a coma who had been hit by an IED. The doctors had performed a craniotomy to relieve pressure on his brain, so his head was completely wrapped in bandages, and the only visible area was from his mouth to just above his eyes. Underneath the bandages, his skull was gone—there was nothing there. There was medical equipment from his chin up to the ceiling, and a nurse stationed on the other side of him.

I heard from the nurse that the soldier wasn't going to make it. She said they were only keeping him alive so that his wife could see him before he died. They were bringing him to Germany and flying her in from the States just so she could say goodbye. My heart sank. I put my hand on the man and for the entire 7-hour flight, I talked to him, thanked him, prayed for him. I told him what was happening, where he was heading, and that he was on his way to see his wife. And on that flight I cried a few times, not only for him and his family, but because I knew that the soldier could have easily been any of the two thousand troops I was about to lead. I needed strength to keep this from happening to anyone under my command, or to cope, lead, and survive in the event it did. I will never forget that flight and the indelible mark it left on my soul, and on my motivation to serve and lead.

Before we deployed overseas, my team and I did one final multiweek exercise in Florida to make sure we were ready. I was able to sneak away one Saturday evening for mass. Before the service began, I closed my eyes tightly and tuned out the rest of the world. I prayed that God would please take care of my people, help me to help them, help me to make great decisions, help me provide sound and principled leadership, and, most important, help me bring everyone safely home.

I finished my silent prayer, and in the very next moment, I opened the mass guide and pre-read the first reading for that mass. It was the story of Solomon, from the first book of Kings: "God said, 'Ask something of me and I will give it you.'" Solomon asks for something not for himself, but for help serving God's people, for help in understanding and governing them.

"Because you have asked for this," God replies in the reading, "not for a long life for yourself, nor for riches, nor for the life of your enemies, but for understanding so that you may know what is right—I do as you requested."

I had literally just made the same prayer that Solomon made—before seeing it on the page—and here, in that final mass before leaving for the unknown, in that very first reading, I felt God speaking directly to me and answering that prayer, offering me the guidance and safety that I was seeking. And sure, skeptics and nonbelievers will see this as mere coincidence—but I absolutely didn't, and that belief helped carry me through the deployment. I carefully tore the page out of the mass book—I hope God can forgive me—and to this day it is stored in my personal Bible as a reminder to orient myself more for others than for myself.

Only a few weeks later, now in Afghanistan, still getting settled, I went to the Saturday mass in my SEAL camp, which was led by an Australian Catholic priest whose SAS (Special Air Service) Force shared our base. The closing prayer was the Irish blessing, about rain falling softly upon the fields. I went back to my room afterward to continue the unpacking I'd slowly started over the course of the week—and in the very first bag I reached into, I found in my hand the mass card from my grandfather's funeral. It had either never been removed from that piece of luggage or had somehow mysteriously found its way in there. When I flipped it over, I saw something that I hadn't remembered was on the back . . . that very same Irish blessing I'd just heard only minutes before. To me, it was yet another sign, providing me assurance that my grandfather was watching over me and over the deployment.

+ + +

One more story: When I turned sixteen, my grandfather offered me what he called "the best present in the world." He handed me a package, and as I peeled away the wrapping paper, I saw a framed sheet of paper, a poem he had typed up for me. At the bottom, he had written: "Michael, my father made me memorize this poem as a young boy because he felt this, above all others, embodied what it means to be a man. I hereby pass this to you and encourage you to turn to these words when things get difficult."

The poem was Rudyard Kipling's "If," which begins:

If you can keep your head when all about you
Are losing theirs and blaming it on you,
If you can trust yourself when all men doubt you,
But make allowance for their doubting too;

If you can wait and not be tired by waiting,
    Or being lied about, don't deal in lies,
Or being hated, don't give way to hating,
    And yet don't look too good, nor talk too wise

I wrote in chapter 2 about the day the Taliban shot six children and blamed it on us and my family member at home was simultaneously having a medical crisis. I was as overwhelmed with stress as I'd ever felt, and reached out to my incredible second-in-command and close friend, Rocky. He promised he would watch out for me.

Not two hours after our conversation, an email from Rocky appeared in my inbox. No words, just a cut-and-paste of that very same Rudyard Kipling poem staring back at me from the screen. No one but my wife, siblings, and parents knew about my grandfather's gift to me twenty-five years earlier. I felt such astonishment and emotion in that moment. For me, it was yet another sign that my grandfather was looking down from above.

+ + +

I never shared these stories with my teammates. I was afraid I'd risk losing the trust I'd built up with those who didn't share my beliefs, that they would somehow see my faith in God as compromising my ability to lead us through the very real dangers we faced, which weren't going to be resolved by divine intervention. I worried they would judge or reject me, and it would hamper my ability to be the most effective Commander I could be. Perhaps I didn't have enough conviction to trust that my beliefs were part of what made me strong—or at least to trust that others would see it that way.

I see things a little differently now, with hindsight. I wish I'd shared more, and I wish others had shared more about the beliefs that kept them focused on what was most important in life. Diversity of faith isn't something we always think about in the same way we think about all the other diversities we need to celebrate, but it's just as critical. Sharing our beliefs with others, baring our truest selves, finding common elements and bonding because of them can be so powerful, especially in the high-stakes environment of battle.

It's not that I think all beliefs are interchangeable. But there are far more elements that tie our beliefs together than divide us. No matter what you call yourself—religious or not, or whichever religion you hold in your heart—virtually all of us can stand up proudly for the ideas of forgiveness, tolerance, respect, putting others before self, trying to be the best person we can be, and living the best life we can live. I don't know that my beliefs are the truest form of truth any more than I can guarantee someone else's aren't. But I do think that having those beliefs, whatever they are, and living by them can bring us all closer to finding meaning in everything we do—and sharing them can bring us closer together.

Do the Things That Are Most Meaningful to You

The first step is to find the beliefs that bring you meaning. The next step is to act on them. There are choices to make every moment of every day. If you mentor underprivileged kids when you instead really want to save the environment, you can force it, but you'll probably lose interest over time, and you won't be as effective as you would have been had you moved in the direction your heart was pushing you. It's okay that some things truly move some of us and some things don't. There are lots of people in the world, and lots of ways to make an impact. We need to find what authentically resonates with each of us as individuals. This requires thinking deeply and being honest with ourselves. The answers that sound right aren't always the ones that feel right. We don't want to take fast trains to the wrong station.

I've dealt with this issue throughout my career. As a White House Fellow, I ultimately knew that national security was where I was most motivated to make an impact. The story that comes to mind here is of my work on President Obama's first true international crisis, dealing with the *Maersk Alabama*, a cargo ship that was hijacked by Somali pirates in the Indian Ocean (the story of which was the inspiration for the movie *Captain Phillips*, starring Tom Hanks). Those days, busy with work in the first few months of President Obama's administration, my BlackBerry was constantly buzzing around the clock. On this particular night, it was buzzing more than normal, and at three a.m., I took a look and saw why: an American ship had been captured by pirates. I immediately snapped to attention. This was reminiscent of when I had been held at gunpoint in Peru, so I knew how the hostages would be feeling, but more important, I realized that this could quickly escalate to an international crisis. I knew that the pirates, motivated by money, would be very happy to have Americans in their grasp, and I also learned that the ship was far enough offshore that it would take a while to get help to it.

I sprang into action and called my friend Chris, a former White House Fellow now in charge of the group of SEALs who were best positioned to act. I knew I was skipping a bunch of levels in the chain of command, but I also knew I had to move quickly and that informal communication to a trusted friend could provide a valuable head start that would increase the probability of mission success. I told Chris he should take a look at the situation and get ready in case an order came his way. By six a.m., I was in my suit and at the Pentagon to meet with the military leadership in the National Military Command Center, the most senior operations center for the Department of Defense, where all national crises are handled. I introduced myself to the three-star General who was serving in a role that was effectively the Chief Operating Officer for the entire Department of Defense, and made it clear that although I was wearing a suit, I was an active Navy SEAL Commander.

It was important for me to establish myself as "one of them." Civilian control of the military is a bedrock of our democracy, but also often a source of tension when one side doesn't fully trust or agree with the other. I asked the General for his message as to how the Department of Defense was going to be handling this situation. I said I needed to bring that message back to the White House. At this point, I was the only person from the White House who had engaged on this issue—I was acting on my own, and wanted to be fully informed so I could make sound recommendations when I raised the issue later that morning—but I didn't want the General to feel like he was answering to me and not to the President, who of course would make any decision associated with a military intervention.

He told me the message was that no military option was being contemplated. I knew he was thinking that as soon as we sent warships to support a private shipping company, we would begin heading down a slippery slope of resource allocation for the private sector, which could get onerous and untenable. But I didn't see it that way. This was not just American lives at risk and an isolated hostage situation, but an initial event that could play out into something much worse. I tried to sway his thinking by asking some carefully worded questions, hoping I could lead him to the same answers I was coming up with in my head, but he wouldn't budge.

I went back across the river to the White House and met with Tom Donilon, Denis McDonough, and Mark Lippert. Tom was the Deputy National Security Advisor, an incredibly sharp man who was always juggling multiple world crises and domestic disagreements. Denis was an energetic, brilliant, and very personable official who later became President Obama's Chief of Staff. Mark was a close friend and incredible human being with firsthand experience as an intelligence officer with the SEALs in Iraq, and the Chief of Staff for the entire National Security Council. I appreciated how each of these men listened to my thinking. I explained that we wanted to avoid using military action, but that it would be irresponsible not to be thinking ahead of the issue, planning for the worst, and directing the Department of Defense to prepare options.

I called the Pentagon and a one-star Admiral who was on duty told me that his guidance was not to prepare any options to deal with the situation. I responded with something I said only twice in my two years in my position at the National Security Council: "Sir, please take this as direction from the White House." I told him that the Department of Defense needed to prepare military options to rescue the crew and keep the pirate captors from selling Captain Phillips to Al-Shabaab or another terrorist organization. "The only question," I said to the Admiral, "is how fast you can have options back to the National Security Council."

By the afternoon, my biggest worry had become real. The pirates had left the ship—putting the crew out of danger—but they had taken Captain Phillips with them, and were holding him hostage on a lifeboat, heading toward shore. Fortunately, by that point the Department of Defense had done what it does best and was giving the National Security Council and the President real options to address a really hard problem.

My friend Scott, Commander of the entire Task Force being deployed for the mission, and Chris, a leader of the tactical response itself, arrived on scene halfway around the globe in a matter of hours after the mission was launched. They averted a crisis on Easter Sunday as they shot three pirates with three rounds in the dark of night while both their ship and the pirates' lifeboat rocked up and down on the swells of the open ocean. Scott, Chris, and their snipers were true heroes that day.

I was personally so proud knowing that I had gotten ahead of the problem despite institutional resistance and made the day easier for everyone involved in the response. I'll always treasure a wonderful, personal handwritten note I got from President Obama on White House stationery. But the thing I was most thankful for was that we did our job and that it went well. This was the first foreign policy showdown for a new administration and it sent a clear message to other pirates and to the world that America is always prepared and ready.

✦ ✦ ✦

After leaving the White House, before I headed to southeastern Afghanistan to lead SEAL Team TWO, I decided it would be meaningful to try to do something to help the spouses that my team and I were about to leave behind. I wanted to relieve some small portion of their stress by getting them a few breaks while we were gone—more specifically, by finding and paying for babysitting hours. This was stress I knew from experience: my wife and daughter had lived through years of my deployments when I went overseas seven times for six months or more. I knew that even ten hours of babysitting each month would make a huge difference in people's lives. I worked to find partners who would be willing to donate money to the Navy SEAL Foundation, a 501(c)(3) charity designed to help SEALs and their families, and I spoke in support of the effort at a few prominent organizations in the New York City finance world. Funds were donated, the program was launched thanks to some wonderful work by the SEAL Foundation, and I went off to Afghanistan, feeling great that all our spouses could spend ten monthly "use or lose" babysitting hours any time or way they deemed best.

What do you feel the greatest about in your life, and how can you do more of that? How can you align your passion to a larger cause? I was so pleased when I was able to help raise the money for babysitting. To do so called on my skills and my connections, opened up new opportunities for me, and also made a real and meaningful difference in people's lives. No one asked me to do it, just like no one's necessarily asking you to do the things you are best positioned to succeed at doing. The hard work is figuring out what the world needs, and how it intersects with what feels most rewarding to you. Figure that out, and actually getting it done becomes the easy part.

This is why I never say that military service is for everyone, and why even as I try to make the case that we all ought to serve in some capacity, I never want to tell anyone how that service should play out. There can be just as much meaning in helping to build a successful business, or a happy family, as there is in military service. The problem is that a lot of people go through life and make choices without thinking about what's most meaningful to them. Sometimes it's because we don't have the bandwidth to slow down and really reflect—the bills have to get paid; the kids have to have food on the table—but sometimes it's simply because we don't do the hard work of figuring it out.

+ + +

I had a lot of time to think about these issues while out in the desert, hungry, lonely, and tired. Deployment can feel awfully boring sometimes. Particularly in media portrayals, we're not often shown the reality of military life in between the gunfights. There are absolutely those moments of dramatic action, but there's also a heck of a lot of sitting, watching, and waiting. When you're out there, you can't help but remember how far you are from your spouse, how you're not helping to raise your children, mow the lawn, or do the grocery shopping. You think about the fact that your spouse and kids are always one fateful second away from getting that visit from a uniformed officer telling them there was an unfortunate event and you didn't make it. Like I've said, I sometimes wondered if I would even know if I was dead, should that IED go off or a gunshot sound from out of nowhere.

To survive in that environment, it has to mean something to you. It has to feel like the sacrifice is worth it. If it doesn't, you're in the wrong place, doing the wrong thing. But that's okay. We need SEALs, but we also need immensely talented people to keep us from needing more SEALs, to do the things that keep us out of war in the first place. We need people whose passions cross the spectrum, because we need people fighting their hardest for every cause out there.

One of the causes I've spent a lot of my time on recently is the National Medal of Honor Museum, for which I'm proud to be a member of the board of directors. I got connected with this museum (which was in the conceptual stage when I got involved, and is still under development) through a friend at Bridgewater, who said that his former officemate at McKinsey could use some advice on a project. The project turned out to be the National Medal of Honor Museum, a tribute to the nation's greatest heroes and the values they've helped to spread around the world.

If you don't know much about the National Medal of Honor, it's America's most revered military decoration, and the stories of the more than 3,500 servicemen and servicewomen who've received them, from the Civil War up through the present day, are extraordinary. One of them is my friend Britt Slabinski ("Slab"), a true hero, whose helicopter was hit by enemy fire, causing fellow SEAL Neil Roberts to fall out of the helicopter and have to fight alone on the ground on an inhospitable mountainside deep in Taliban-infested territory. Slab's helicopter crash-landed, and he led his team back up the mountain on a mission to rescue Neil and neutralize the Taliban, a mission they knew might end with fatal results. Slab's Medal of Honor citation reads as they all do—like fiction from an unbelievable movie.

Scrolling through a list of Medal of Honor recipients and what they did to receive that recognition would make anyone feel truly in awe of the bravery that exists throughout this country. Rescuing hostages, running toward suicide bombers, diving for active grenades, risking their lives to provide medical aid to their teammates—and the chance to share those stories with the broader public, to inspire others to understand the qualities of heroism and spread those values throughout our great nation is something that gets me excited whenever I think about it. It's projects like these that give my life special purpose and meaning, just like there are projects we all can find that strike us at our core and motivate us to do the hard work to make things happen. If you're ever having trouble figuring out what is most meaningful to you or what kinds of goals you ought to be chasing, think about what you would do if you could spend your time doing anything you wanted. The activities and causes to which you naturally gravitate are the best places to start searching for opportunities to contribute.

As of this writing, we recently selected a site for the museum in Arlington, Texas, just steps from the venues the Dallas Cowboys and Texas Rangers call home. I can't wait for it to open and for these stories to become more widely appreciated.

You Can Never Know the Future, so Make the Best Decision for Now

One of my bigger career disappointments happened way back in 2000 while I was serving in Kosovo. I had applied to SEAL Team SIX, convinced that it would be the best path to continue to contribute to the SEALs and the nation. At the time, SEAL Team SIX was the likeliest route to serving in combat, and I thought I needed that experience to grow as a SEAL. I was one of four SEAL officers chosen for the team that year, and was thrilled to have the opportunity. And then my Commanding Officer decided not to let me come home from Kosovo three weeks early to be part of the team's training class, so I couldn't join. There was no way around it, no exceptions, no way to make it work. It felt so unfair that one officer could stand in my way even after I'd been chosen. I was so frustrated at the rigid hierarchy, the rules and procedures, the way I didn't have full control over my career path. I told myself that I should quit the Navy, get out, do something else.

And maybe I should have. I don't know how my life would have unfolded had I left the SEALs in 2000. I did know at the time that I shouldn't make a big decision like that when emotions were high, and certainly not at the end of a long, exhausting deployment. President Lincoln's library contains many letters he wrote but never sent, letters detailing his frustration with his generals during the Civil War that he wrote to process his feelings but never signed and had no intention of sending. Time to calmly reflect will inevitably lead to a better decision, in any area.

Indeed, after I'd had a chance to think it over, I realized that the Navy was still where I wanted to be. Even if I thought I was sacrificing my future, we can never really know what will happen. All we can do is make the best decision for now. At the time, I thought I'd never get the combat experience I was hoping for. And then, after 9/11, we all got involved in far more combat than we ever wanted or expected to—and I realized how naïve so many of us in the military are to be looking for that kind of experience in the first place. Once you have real combat experience, you realize it's nothing to wish for. My point is that we can't plan our lives ten steps ahead. We can't know how things will unfold. We can only make the right move given what we know at that moment.

+ + +

As a White House Fellow, one of the privileges I enjoyed was getting to meet and be mentored by national leaders—from the public, nonprofit, and private sectors. I had the opportunity to hear from so many successful men and women about how they had ended up in their positions, and what wisdom they wanted to pass down to the next generation. The common thread, despite the very different paths these professionals had taken, was that no one had been able to effectively plan their careers over the long term. They excelled at what they were doing, and opportunities—whether expected or unexpected—found them, or the desire for new opportunities developed within them. If you say that you know what you are going to be doing in five, ten, or fifteen years, I say you're either lying to yourself or you're going to be proven wrong.

I've heard lots of times that my own résumé looks awfully strange, between the SEALs and the White House and now the business world. The thread that ties it all together is that I've leaned into the hardest situations I could find, rolled my sleeves up, and tried to learn and contribute as well as I could. I went to Bridgewater because it had the smartest people I could find, and I knew I would learn an incredible amount. I also knew that my past experiences would matter there, and would truly help the company, because Bridgewater is constantly seeking fresh ideas.

After Bridgewater, I moved to Cognizant and had the great privilege of working with Frank D'Souza, who became a close and trusted friend. Moving to Cognizant, I had to draw on my experiences to navigate areas that were at first entirely new to me, from dealing with an activist investor—a true crisis for a public company—to working on a variety of initiatives to take the company to the next level of growth. When I started, I felt like I was constantly learning something new, but at the same time using my past experiences to make important contributions to the firm's success.

I've learned over time that organizations already know what they know and are full of subject matter experts in whatever it is that they do. The thing that is often missing is external perspective and the ability to bring in fresh ideas from outside the business that can potentially grow top-line revenue or help the company cut costs and increase profit. While I didn't grow up as a technologist, leading a large group of people serving clients, and helping them run and change their business is really just a test of vision, leadership, and trust. Good processes and good decision-making are effective no matter the context, and finding success in one role takes pretty much the same skills as finding success in any other role. It's all about who you are and how you approach the world; the details can be learned.

To that end: Worry first about building the foundation of your life, and build the walls and the roof later. Grow foundational skills, and they will help you no matter where you find yourself. Do amazing work, in whatever capacity you can, and opportunities will follow. Too often, we think about life as a zero-sum game, with winners and losers. But it's not. We can all be winners. We can all lift each other up. There are roles for all of us, and we can create our own opportunities if we can't find the right one out there. Achievement is not limited to a small group of people. The more people who succeed, the more people who are available to create a world ready for even more success.

Besides, we change. The choices we make now aren't necessarily ones that we have to live with forever. The more you try, the more you know, and the more you learn about yourself and what drives you. We can be great at something, and then decide to make a shift. We can reinvent ourselves, change careers, change our lives. Because we can't know or fully plan the future, it's incumbent on us to do what we can all the time, not just wait until all the pieces are in place. All the pieces will never be in place. Things don't get done unless we actually start to do them.

I've interviewed more than a thousand people for important, high-paying, high-impact jobs. I've talked them through their processes for figuring out whether to make the move. I tell them to be honest with themselves about the person they are, not the person they wish they could be. A role can sound perfect on paper, but if it doesn't fit, you can't force it. We have to respect the voices inside our hearts, which rarely lead us astray. We have to understand what gives us energy—not just what we're good at.

+ + +

I started to figure some of this out back in college at Holy Cross. When you think about a Jesuit liberal arts education, the goal is to figure out who (not what) you are going to be in life. You try things out along the way, test what you like, and see what sticks. People are rarely shy with advice—this entire book is no exception—but everyone who offers advice has their own biases. Recognize these biases (including mine), and take what you can from what people tell you. Apply what fits and discard the rest. Over time, you figure out who you are, what drives you, and the change you want to bring to the world. You figure out what it means to you to succeed. Because success means something different to each of us, and it's often very personal.

In Afghanistan, our medical unit was often treating people outside the SEALs, whether from other branches of the US military or, when we had capacity, the Afghans training with us. Rich, my peer in the Army, was running a Green Beret special operations force responsible for the southern part of Afghanistan, and his team would often request the use of our medical unit, because it was frequently the closest one to the battlefield where the need would emerge. One night, he called me and said a group of his men had been hit by an IED, and one of his junior guys, Anthony, was badly impacted—"his bell was rung," Rich said, meaning that he suspected Anthony had a concussion and wanted the doctors to take a look.

I went down to see Anthony at about three in the morning, as soon as I was able to step away from the operations center. He looked as if he'd been hit full-frontal by an NFL linebacker, but he talked as if there wasn't a scratch on him. The doctors told me that the question of whether to pull him from his team could go either way. "It's not a situation where we'd mandate his evacuation," they told me. If we wanted to be ultra-cautious, we could send him to Kandahar for further evaluation and then likely off to Germany for a full workup. He could potentially be sent home from there. Alternatively, the doctors would fully support skipping the workup and returning Anthony to his team.

It was my call, so what I felt I needed to evaluate in that situation was Anthony's state of mind. Regardless of his physical condition, was he mentally ready to jump back in? If I had any doubt in these situations, I would act conservatively, every time;

I'd rather the doctors check for a traumatic brain injury and do a more thorough assessment. If this was a clear case, it would have been easy. I had to talk to Anthony.

As I introduced myself, Anthony told me this was actually the second time in two weeks that this had happened to him. He'd been blown up just fourteen days earlier and had wanted to rejoin his team afterward. I felt like that was going to make it an easy call—there was no way he should be sent back again, with a second possible brain injury just two weeks after the first. I told him he definitely didn't have to repeat what had happened before. I could easily get him flown to Germany for the full workup, and make sure he was absolutely okay. Two near-death incidents within two weeks and he might very well get sent home, I told him.

At first, he gave me the reflexive soldier answer—"Sir, I want to be back with my team as soon as possible." I knew I needed to get deeper than that answer and figure out what was real and true. Around four a.m., I walked with Anthony to my office, through the moonless night, carrying his rifle, helmet, and operational gear for him, his discomfort clear, as he was a junior enlisted soldier and I was the Commanding Officer (a difference that is hard to understand in the civilian world but that means so much in military hierarchy). I carried his gear in order to make it clear to him that I was on his side, and that this wasn't going to be the typical interaction that a lower-ranking soldier would have with an officer. I wanted us—I *needed* us—to have a real, honest conversation.

Sitting in my office, I told Anthony for a second time that he didn't have to go right back to his team. I explained that he didn't have to put on a brave face, and assured him that coming this close to death—twice, and in such a short span of time—would make anyone, even me, hesitant to get right back out there.

Anthony opened up and shared his thoughts, then sat straight up, looked me in the eye, and said, "Sir, I mean every word I'm saying. I am here to support my team and fight for a cause greater than self. My team is weaker without me, and I don't want to let that happen. These aren't just words, they're my true feelings. Please, sir, send me back to my unit." He said it with such emphasis and real emotion, I couldn't help but be convinced.

I was dumbfounded, amazed, blown away by his attitude. I paused, searching for the right words, then finally locked eyes with him and asked him, "Anthony, what's a hero?" He paused as if it was a trick question, but I didn't mean it that way, so I jumped in to fill the silence. "You," I told him, with deep sincerity and respect. "You are a hero. Two near-death experiences and you want to be right back in there, serving your country and your teammates. Your team and the nation are lucky to have you." Anthony knew how he wanted to serve his country, and he knew where he found meaning in his life. I agreed to let him return to his team.

A couple of weeks later, Rich called me—there was a mass casualty situation, "green on blue," he said. This code meant that a team of Army Special Forces had been attacked by members of an Afghan troop that was being trained by the US. The Afghan troop had been infiltrated by the Taliban, and now they were shooting Americans. There was at least one soldier killed in action, Rich said, and three others badly wounded. I told him to send me the wounded and we would do everything we could.

The injured men arrived, and two of them were completely out of it on painkillers by that point, but the third was able to speak and wanted me to know what had happened. He told me that in the chaos of the shooting, one American teammate had stepped forward to put himself in harm's way. He bravely killed the shooter before the man could do any further damage, sacrificing his own life but in the process saving no small number of his teammates from being shot and killed. He was a real hero. I told this guy that I didn't think I knew anyone from his unit, but I asked the name of the hero nevertheless.

It was Anthony.

When the wounded soldier said Anthony's name, I had such a swirl of mixed feelings. I was devastated, of course, that he'd lost his life. I felt responsible, that I'd been the one to send him back into the field. And I felt so thankful that he had been there to step up and save his teammates. In the aftermath, I asked myself if I'd made the right call. Had I let a soldier's passion sway my decision, and ultimately cost him his life? I don't know, I really don't. But I knew that Anthony wouldn't have let me make a different decision. I felt, and still feel, such respect and gratitude for this soldier who knew, with no ambiguity, how he wanted to make a difference in the world, and what gave his life meaning. We all should strive for such clarity.

+ + +

Finding meaning as individuals really is all about asking ourselves the hardest questions and figuring out what moves us, what motivates us, what compels us to act. For me, it's in large part my faith, which informs my desire to serve and to help.

But it's also my commitment to my team and my teammates. This chapter was all about finding meaning and strength for ourselves—and in the next chapter, we'll move on to the team, and talk about how a focus on others and a "Never Enough" attitude toward impacting their lives can also bring tremendous meaning and fulfillment to our own journeys.

CHAPTER 8

WE LIVE AND DIE FOR PEOPLE, NOT CAUSES

Meaning in the Bonds We Build with Others

had been home from Afghanistan for just a few weeks when I found out that my replacement as Commander of the Special Operations Task Force, who had taken over when my team finished its deployment, had decided to take his own life, shooting himself with his pistol in his room, in the bed I had slept in for the previous ten months.

I was shocked and devastated. He and I were good friends, former roommates, BUD/S classmates twenty years earlier. We had come up the ranks together. Before we each got married and started our families, we shared a house in Virginia Beach for three years. We were inseparable in those days. We had bonded over our mutual frustration at the pull-up bar during BUD/S training. One Saturday morning, after we'd both failed the day before to come anywhere close to matching the 15 to 20 pull-ups our fellow trainees were able to do, we decided to go find

a pull-up bar to practice on, far away from the BUD/S compound, where no one would stumble upon us. Despite a full
night's sleep, we were still struggling. As we each fought through
our fourth pull-up, I can still see his face and hear the chuckle in
his voice as he turned to me and said, "World's finest, right here."

He was loyal, genuine, a man who could find humor in absolutely anything. Another time in training, we were so cold
on a boat ride back to the compound after an icy swim that we
found ourselves fighting over where to place one rubber fin that
was shielding (very small) parts of us from the 40-knot winds.
There we were, two grown adults—SEAL trainees—fighting
over a tiny rubber fin to help make us a tiny bit warmer and just a
drop less miserable. We stopped for a moment and realized what
we were fighting over, and we both just broke out in hysterical
laughter. It seemed like we were always laughing back then.

When I was deployed, he would check in on my family, and
when he was deployed, I would check in on his. I would say that
I trusted him with my life, except that it was so much more than
that. As SEALs, we have no choice but to trust everyone on our
team with our life, every minute of every day on the battlefield.
But when you bond with someone, it's not so much about trusting them with your life—it's about wanting them to be there in
the trenches with you, feeling better because you know they're
right alongside you. He was so much more than a fellow SEAL.
He was a friend, a teammate, a brother, a shining example of the
bravery a human being can exhibit.

As the outgoing and incoming commanders, we were the
last on our respective teams to rotate, as it always goes when
one SEAL Team replaces another. The transition is always a
complex process fraught with risk. First we would rotate the out-

stations, the outposts throughout the region located away from headquarters. We would ease people in and out over the course of a few weeks, so that the new SEALs could learn from the old ones what was and wasn't working, who to trust, and what the day-to-day of the deployment looked like. This was the standard way of mitigating as much risk as possible while rotating forces.

Finally, the top officers would make their switch. For two weeks, just a few months before he died, my friend and I got to be teammates again, sharing responsibilities and doing everything together. I showed him how I set my vision, worked to achieve it, and chose our operations. I introduced him to the Afghan political and military officials who were most helpful to our cause, told him who should be watched closely and who was likely in bed with the Taliban. I showed him what routes needed to be avoided in order to minimize the chance of roadside bombs, what elements of our operations were working and what we were struggling with, and the logistics behind getting enough gas, food, and water.

There was one day toward the end of the transition when I went to say goodbye to one of the villages my team and I had become particularly involved with during the deployment. The villagers were celebrating us, and expressing their thanks for our help. I introduced my friend to the Afghans who lived there, and explained that he would be continuing our efforts and carrying our great relationship forward. The villagers unexpectedly embraced us both, wrapped us in their traditional clothing, and honored us for the work we had done and the work yet to come. I distinctly remember my friend and I walking back to the helicopter, both of us still wearing the traditional headgear they had given us as a gift. He was embarrassed—he wasn't used to this, and he'd done nothing yet to deserve the honor—but I had confidence he'd grow to feel the same kind of bond and connection with the people we were helping as I had over the previous months.

Finally, the transition was complete, and I found myself on the last flight home with about two dozen of my fellow key leaders and staff. I never saw my friend again.

+ + +

He and I had daughters around the same age, which made our continued bond over the years that much more special. My daughter, knowing what it was like to have a father overseas for months, knowing the fear and loneliness the deployment involved, made his daughter a present and sent it to her right before her father left for Afghanistan. On 270 notecards, one for each day of the deployment, my daughter wrote a message, a little inspiration so my friend's daughter wouldn't feel like her father was so far away. "When you miss your dad, take a T-shirt from his drawer, put it on, and pretend you're getting a hug from him," one of the cards read. They were all like that, unique and special ideas to keep his daughter feeling connected to her dad.

The gift made me, as a father, feel so proud. I didn't tell my daughter to do it. No one did. She was in sixth grade at the time, and put the gift together with no direction from my wife or me at all—but I have to tell you, as special as I know my wife and daughter are, the reality is that military families do things like this for each other all the time. Within the military community, there was nothing particularly extraordinary about it. People on the outside don't see the kind of bonds that get formed through such shared sacrifice. Our families do so much for each other, and it all ties back to the principles I'll talk about in this chapter, about reaching out, and about taking action to help each other.

I hadn't seen my daughter's deployment box until the night my friend died, when I, along with another SEAL friend who was very close to the family, went to their house to be with his wife and daughter and help them process the news. I still remember hearing the screams from the other room as my fellow SEAL broke the news to their daughter. "He promised me he would come home!" she shrieked. "He promised me he would come home!"

We had talked to a child psychologist by phone in the car on the way, asking, "Do we tell his daughter the truth of what happened now, or do we wait until she's older and might be able to better understand it?" The psychologist said we had no choice but to tell her now. It was such an awful moment, this family's life forever altered—and there was nothing we could do to change that reality.

I will always wonder if I could have done more to help my friend and prevent the tragedy of his death. I don't know that there was anything I could have said to him that would have stopped him from making the decision he did, but I have to admit that I'm full of regret about one particular choice I made. The day before he killed himself, I actually picked up the phone to call him, just to check in and see how he was doing. As I dialed, I remembered there was a new policy requiring a 4-digit PIN to be able to get through on my secure military line, and I didn't have one. Given that it was a Friday afternoon and few people were at work to help, I decided I would just call on Monday. I never got the chance.

It would be awfully presumptuous of me to assume that I might have had the magic words on that call to get through to him and help him understand what a horrific choice he was about to make, but I do know that I was one of the few people alive who might have been able to detect a problem or a worry in his voice, and beyond that, I was one of the few people in a position to potentially get him help. I use the experience as a reminder to never get complacent in my relationships with friends and family, to never think I've done enough for someone, and to always make an effort to be sure I'm hearing their truest thoughts and feelings and doing what I can to support them. There are three principles I live by in this area: to be intrusive in people's lives, to be a do-er rather than a be-er, and to push to have real impact on those around me. They're each so critical to finding meaning in our bonds with others.

Be Intrusive in People's Lives

We often hear "intrusive" as a negative word, and maybe sometimes it is. We don't want to overstep people's boundaries, make them uncomfortable, or push past the point of politeness in our interactions. But I think we need to reframe intrusion as something critically necessary to having meaningful relationships. We have to be willing to intrude, to ask the hard questions and have the hard conversations—or we're not really making a difference. It's natural to stick to your agenda, especially in a professional setting. Someone might be struggling, but as long as they're doing the work, you tell yourself it's none of your business. But it is our business if we might be able to help. Small talk is easy, but getting someone to be vulnerable, emotional, and honest can be hard. And yet without those deeper conversations, we can never really get to know each other.

As a leader in the SEALs, I wanted to be the kind of person

others knew they could turn to when things got tough. In life, I strive to be that kind of person for everyone I know. None of what we do—no matter how excellent or agile we train ourselves to become—really matters if we lack the meaning that comes from our bonds and relationships.

In the business world, one of the biggest disappointments I see is the way that networking is often seen as a transactional relationship—what can I get from someone else? Real networking comes from investing energy in other people, giving more than taking, without thinking about whether you'll ever get paid back. I've found that amazing results can emerge from genuinely giving to others and serving them however you can.

First, you feel great about it. Second, the people you help now will inevitably end up helping you later, in ways you can't plan for or predict. You can't put in the time with an eye toward your ultimate rewards, but trust me, those rewards will come, especially in your own times of need. The people you invest in without an expectation of investment in return will be the first people who help you whenever it is they can. They are the ones who will say yes to a favor before you even finish asking for one. They are the ones who will praise you to the world and bring unexpected opportunities your way.

There is no shortcut. When I worked in the White House, the days were exceedingly long. There was always so much more work to do. But I made it a point three times a week to have lunch with someone new—to get to know them, and to listen to their stories and goals. I went into every lunch knowing that I would learn something, and figuring that there might be a way to do something great together, provide a useful connection, or see a way to offer them help now or in the future.

There is nothing unique about what I did. Anyone can do it—you find the intersection of your needs and theirs, and see if you can work together to bring something great into the world. As a result of those lunchtime conversations, I would learn a few things about the person. First, I would start to understand what they cared about, the highest-impact items on his or her agenda. Second, I would realize what we had in common, the interests and values we shared, the ideas that could bring us together. Third, I would often end up discovering unexpected connections and hidden opportunities.

The way you get to that third point is often through what I think of as expanding the surface area of a discussion, taking it to subjects that might otherwise go unexplored. You often don't know someone's passions or feelings until you happen to stumble upon them. You never know when you might land on a topic that could spark excitement for both of you.

Usually, on the way to those lunches, I'd be thinking about the hundred things I should have been doing at my desk instead. On the way back, all I'd be thinking about was the person I'd just met and the human connection we'd made. At the end of my day, I could never have told you what that extra hour of work would have accomplished, but I could always point to the incredible value of getting to know people in parts of the organization I would not have normally seen. It made me a far more effective leader, with relationships throughout the government—relationships that paid off when I needed to quickly get something onto someone's desk or to reach out for an internal favor.

＋ ＋ ＋

The fact that these connections helped make me better at my job was a wonderful bonus, but the underlying motivation was relationship building and the intent to give more than I was ever going to receive. It wasn't just an attitude I had in the White House. I tried to connect with as many of my SEALs as possible, at every stage of my career. I tried to be as intrusive as I could, like when I fought for two of my SEALs to be picked for an officer training program, spending hours on their recommendation letters and doing whatever I could to advance their applications. A simple story that comes to mind is about Jed, a new SEAL who found himself set to become certified as a military freefall parachutist.

The certification process is different now, but when I was moving up in the ranks, it was incredibly hard to get a spot in freefall parachute training class. There were five or six slots per team per year—for a hundred SEALs. People were forced to wait until their third, fourth, fifth year of service before getting this valuable qualification. Todd, a good friend of mine and an incredibly impressive SEAL, had just served as an instructor at freefall school, and came back to our team explaining that there was a little-known alternative path to becoming certified. As an instructor, Todd could sponsor a "challenge course," and bring twenty SEALs to Yuma, Arizona, to get certified by completing their US Parachute Association "B license" and then doing ten military jumps in three days. We got it right on the calendar.

I asked the team for volunteers to fill our class, and hands went up right away, including Jed's. The very next day, I happened to hear that Jed's wife was pregnant, and that she was likely to give birth right when we'd be off in Arizona getting certified. I could have done nothing—Jed had volunteered for the class, and I could have just ignored what I'd heard and decided that he was allowed to make his own decisions about his life.

Instead, I got intrusive. I went and found Jed, and told him what I'd heard. "Do you really want to miss your child's birth for freefall training?" I asked. He didn't really give me a convincing answer. He said he wanted to be parachute certified, but I could tell he felt conflicted. (It was a very different feeling than I'd had when Anthony told me he wanted nothing more than to rejoin his team after his second near-death experience on the battlefield.) I told Jed I was making the decision for him. "You have your entire life to get freefall certified, but only one day to see your baby born. You're not coming on this trip. You'll thank me later, I promise."

I expected pushback, but what I got was a sigh of relief. "Mr. Hayes," Jed said, "there is nothing I want more than to be at my child's birth. I'm just trying to be a good new guy, and raise my hand for everything, because that's what good new guys do."

Jed still thanks me for making sure he didn't miss one of the most important days of his life just to go jump from an airplane. This is what being intrusive gets you—trust, respect, and the knowledge that you're bettering the lives of people around you. Jed's done a thousand jumps since then, has been freefall certified forever—and is a proud and involved father. He could have given me a different answer, and I'm sure I would have let him go to the training class if that was really what he wanted—but I knew it was important to ask the question, and then to really listen to the answer, beyond just hearing the words. It was important to care.

Be a Do-er, Not a Be-er

Being intrusive is the first step, but it's not the only one. Listening can only get you so far. Sometimes you also need to act. I've found in life that there are people who want to be things—important, rich, powerful, famous, the people carrying the big titles and outsize reputations—and there are also people who simply get up each morning and do things. Be-ers love the title, the shine, and the spotlight. Do-ers get things done.

And you have to get things done in order to truly impact the lives of others. We all want to *be* a good friend. But we don't all act in a way that recognizes that being a good friend means actually doing concrete things that make a difference in our friends' lives, often at a cost to ourselves.

My friend Brian was killed by a roadside bomb on a mission in 2004, during the early phase of the Afghanistan war. He left behind his parents and seven siblings in Boston, all of them huge Red Sox fans. I was in graduate school at Harvard at the time, just across the Charles River, a stone's throw from the famous Green Monster and the world-famous Citgo sign hanging over Fenway Park. When I heard about what happened to Brian, I had a bit of a vision. I could imagine Brian's picture on the scoreboard, his strong, Boston-bred family on the field, and the crowd giving a standing ovation, celebrating Brian's service to the country and to the world.

Nice idea, but I needed to figure out how to make it happen.

I found a way to get connected to a prominent Boston sportswriter, who, after hearing Brian's story, was willing to put me in touch with the Red Sox front office. I talked to an executive there who agreed to run the idea up the chain of command. Through many phone calls, and lots of hard work and coordination, we made my initial vision a reality. Brian's parents and seven siblings stood on the pitcher's mound in front of a standing-room-only crowd of 37,000 at Fenway Park. Brian's father threw out the first pitch and the family was recognized and honored by the team with a three-minute-long standing ovation. Just as the applause started to fade, it picked right back up again and grew even louder.

Seeing Brian's father holding the Navy SEAL flag and watching his family members cry and bask in the applause for their fallen hero made my own tears flow. I'd never seen anything like it, and the pride Brian's family felt as his sacrifice was recognized and cheered right there in their community, in a place they all loved, was so inspiring. It's one of the things in my life that I'm most proud to have helped make happen.

+ + +

A few years later, when I was working in the White House, I helped accomplish something else that was very special. This time, I relied on a close friend and incredible American, Jared Weinstein, President George W. Bush's special assistant and "body man." The SEALs had spent eight years sacrificing tremendously during the Bush administration. After 9/11, the state of the world changed dramatically, and the roles that the SEALs had to play grew vastly more dangerous. I knew it would mean something for the SEALs to hear President Bush's appreciation for the risks they had taken, in person, directly from the Commander in Chief himself. There is so much power in a simple "thank you," to put more gas in all our proverbial tanks, to energize and motivate us to continue our hard, important work.

At the same time, I thought it would be a beautiful gesture for the President to hear from the SEALs how much we valued his leadership during that rough stretch of American history. No matter anyone's personal politics, everyone could agree that President Bush had put in long days in the service of our nation, and I both admired him and knew from Jared how much the President valued the SEALs and our service. He loved hearing stories of military bravery, and meeting young heroes in the armed forces. And yet, as with almost any leader, I imagined that he didn't hear appreciation for his work nearly as often as he heard criticism and complaints. People at the top in any organization only get certain kinds of feedback. From the inside, they get their ego fed, but they rarely hear honest reactions to their performance. From the outside, in almost all cases, they get so much negativity, no matter what the reality is.

I had an idea involving Bush's last official trip as President. He was scheduled to fly to Norfolk and christen an aircraft carrier being named for his father (the USS *George H.W. Bush*). I suggested to Jared that we could get the President to swing over to visit SEAL Team TEN, which was based in Virginia Beach, and we could get the entire East Coast SEAL community together for a private event where President Bush could thank them for their service and the SEALs could thank him for his leadership.

Jared helped to make it happen, and it turned out to be a wonderful, emotional celebration on all sides. I was so proud to be the guy who helped the SEALs meet the President and the President meet the SEALs. It was actually the first time in history that a SEAL Team got to meet a sitting President on its home base, and host an event for the entire community.

As an aside, I got to fly on Air Force One that day, on President Bush's very last trip, and I had the privilege of flying in the presidential helicopter as we flew into Landing Zone (LZ) Green, the helicopter landing area just outside the East Coast SEAL headquarters. From the air as we approached, my mind flashed back to the hundreds of incredibly hard training exercises I had conquered with my closest friends in some of the best and worst conditions along those miles of beach, the obstacle courses, and the grounds. We landed on the same drop zone onto which I had rappelled down fifteen years earlier when I first learned how to rappel out of a helicopter. I'll never forget the emotions I felt seeing the camp come into view, now coming in with the President, so many years later. It forced me to reflect on my life, and I was flooded with gratitude for the experiences I'd been fortunate enough to have, and lucky enough to make it through.

+ + +

That emotional reward I felt came from doing, not just being. Those good feelings come from putting in the work and effort to think of what you'd like to see happen in the world, and then figuring out how to make it so, planning and executing to get it done. The third step is to make sure that those things you're ready to do are in fact the things that will have the maximum impact on the people around you.

Have Real Impact on Those Around You

I want to start with what may feel like a small, insignificant example—but then I want to explain why it's not. In 2007, before my SEAL Team deployed to Iraq, I stood in front of the team and talked about something that I'm not sure any commander had ever brought to the attention of his SEALs: life insurance. I told them I'd done some research, and the military benefit to surviving family members in the case of someone being killed in action, while generous, was probably not enough to satisfy the needs of most families.

For no more than the price of a few cups of coffee a week, I knew that anyone on my team could get more than twice as much term life coverage. I made it clear that of course we knew we were all planning on coming back alive, but there are always risks, and no one deploys without knowing those risks are very real—and that this increased insurance could enable their families to pay off a mortgage, to afford to take some time to figure out life without them, and to not have the stress of financial instability piled on top of all the other stresses the situation would introduce. I maintained that the cost would be worth it.

The team listened, and I didn't think any more about it as we deployed. And then, midway through the deployment, three men from my SEAL Team were killed in action. These weren't men under my command—the team had been split in two when we deployed, some sent with our SEAL colleagues from the West Coast to Anbar Province, which was where I served as Deputy Commander, and some to Baghdad, under the command of a different set of leaders. But I knew the three men well, and I felt just horrible about it. I was woken up with a knock on my door in the middle of the night to be told the news—"Three KIA" (killed in action)—and then I waited an eternity to find out their names and discover which of my friends were no longer with us. For the rest of the deployment I flinched quickly awake every time I heard anything that sounded like knocking. I was living in what was basically a shipping container, 20 feet long, 6 feet wide, 6 feet high, with an air-conditioning unit hooked up through a power cable running around the outside of the structure. The wind would blow the power cable, and I'd jolt up from a sound sleep, thinking it was one of those knocks at the door.

I wouldn't have said that it felt stressful when I was there—I might have called it annoying—but as I reflect back, I realize that there was so much that didn't register as stress at the time, that I didn't allow to register as stress, but that was, in fact, incredibly stressful. While we were in combat, so many of us would have said that we didn't feel the emotions, we were just doing our jobs—but with the benefit of time and hindsight, I know so many people who, when asked if they have any lingering post-traumatic effects, have said things like "I only sleep two nights a week," or "That deployment broke me." We had to push it down deep inside in order to keep moving forward, but it can sometimes hit with full force much later on.

One of the SEALs who was killed in action that day was a friend of mine, Jackson. I couldn't go to his funeral, and I didn't know his family well, and I hadn't checked in on them the way I should have, the way I did for most of the people I knew who were hurt or killed overseas. I saw Jackson's wife at a memorial service for another SEAL a few years after Jackson was killed, and I wanted to approach her. Honestly, I wasn't sure if I should. I didn't know if I would trigger any negative emotions, or do more harm than good. Jackson hadn't been directly under my watch when he died—but he would always be a part of my team, so I felt a great deal of regret and responsibility for his death.

I decided to go up to her and tell her there were some things

I'd wanted to reach out and say to her for years. I wanted her to know how much I missed Jackson, and how sorry I was for not being better about checking in on her, or doing more to help her and her family. But before I could get my words out, she said that she was the one who had wanted to reach out to me all these years, that there was something she wanted to tell me but didn't feel like she could until some time had passed after Jackson's death.

I got ready to spring into action, anticipating an ask and ready to run through walls to help her however I could—to be the do-er I assumed she needed. But she didn't want anything from me. Instead, she said she wanted to thank me because Jackson had taken out the life insurance policy I had recommended, and while of course she would do anything to have Jackson back, that decision had allowed her to be a mom to her kids, to live the life he would have wanted for them instead of being panicked about paying the bills. She had worried for years that admitting the insurance was meaningful would make her sound greedy or focused on the wrong things, but she also knew what a concrete difference it had made for her family.

This is what I mean by impact: things we do that have a real, tangible, concrete effect on the people around us. When my SEALs ask for recommendation letters, connections, help getting into graduate school or getting a job, I could see these as bottom-of-my-list requests that are only going to take me away from my own work, but I don't. I know how meaningful those things can be, so I jump into action and invest as much energy as I can to help.

Incidentally, people know when you care and when you're just doing the minimum to satisfy a request like that. I've asked my SEALs for recommendation letters, too. When I applied to the White House Fellows program, I needed three letters. I suspected then—and know now, from being on the other side of the process—that most people look for the most senior, most experienced, most well-known people who can recommend them, brand-name endorsements from top-tier leaders. I took a different approach. I asked two subordinates to write on my behalf. I went to my top-performing SEALs and told them what I was applying for, and asked for a letter. I told them to be brutally honest about my leadership.

I wanted my letters to reflect real knowledge of my character and my work far better than they would if I had asked someone higher up the chain in the Pentagon who had met me perhaps a handful of times, in situations where I was focused on making the best impression. If you're proud of the way you live your life, there's no reason to worry that the people who know you best won't also be your very best advocates. If this makes you question whether you would feel comfortable relying on an honest recommendation letter written by one of your subordinates, you ought to reflect on whether you're doing enough and helping the people under you as much as you can.

+ + +

One of the people who had the most impact on my life was Senior Chief McClatchy, one of my BUD/S instructors during SEAL training. McClatchy was mean as hell, and hard as they come, gruff, uber intense, and phenomenally frightening. My buddy Job and I were terrified of him—one time, Job fell asleep during a class in dive physics, and McClatchy literally pulled him over the desk and made him do a seemingly endless number of push-ups and star-jumpers (the SEAL term for jumping as high into the air as you can, again and again, with no rest between jumps).

I joined SEAL Team FOUR after graduation as an ensign (the lowest officer rank). McClatchy was now a platoon chief. He pulled me aside one day and said, "I'm going to give you something that you had better have on you for the rest of your time here. If I ever ask you for it and you don't have it, I will make BUD/S seem like it was a vacation."

I had no idea what he was about to hand me. And then he softened his tone, stepped toward me, and unfolded a piece of paper listing the names of every SEAL in my platoon. He said, "Keep their names in your pocket, so that every waking minute of every day you keep in mind that the lives of these men depend on you."

I've never forgotten that list, or that everything I did as a SEAL had the possibility of affecting the lives of every other person on my team.

✦ ✦ ✦

Impacting the lives of others is how we bring meaning to our own life. When I give talks, I tell the story of Mitch, as I did back in chapter 4, the SEAL who moved forward amid heavy gunfire to save his teammate Luke. I talk about the tactical aspects of his decision—how he did it, how he knew when to step forward and when to step back—but I also talk about *why* he did it, and what drives people to take extraordinary risks in missions like these. When asked to reflect on this, the answers I hear from audiences are varied, but most center on the idea of fighting for a cause: for America, for patriotism, for democracy, for contributing to something larger than self. But as important as all those factors are, I believe the reason that someone moves forward in a gunfight is because they care deeply about their teammates, not because they're thinking about their abstract values. Especially when the stakes are so high, we die for people, not causes.

After being injured in the field, Mitch was sent home from our deployment, and I didn't see him again until months later, when I was back at my SEAL Team headquarters in Virginia finishing up some post-deployment duties. I went out for a beach run one morning, and as I was passing through the 10-foot fence separating headquarters from the rest of the world, I suddenly saw Mitch, running toward me from the other direction. I couldn't believe my eyes. Last I had seen, he was nearly dead. And now, just a few months later, he had recovered spectacularly. We gave each other a hug and caught up on what we'd each missed.

It was almost overwhelmingly emotional for me to see him again, after knowing the extent of his injuries. As he ran off and I got around the corner, out of sight, I sat down on the sand and couldn't stop the tears. We all need to feel overwhelmed sometimes. It's proof that our bonds are strong, our relationships real.

✦ ✦ ✦

One final story about impact: When I went to Harvard for graduate school in 2003, I had literally no obligations to the Navy for the two years I was there to study. I was the first SEAL to get this privilege—the Navy selected one officer per year as a "politico-military fellow," awarded two years of fully funded graduate school. The fellowship had always gone to ship drivers, pilots, or submariners—and as the first SEAL ever chosen, I felt so fortunate to have the opportunity. As soon as I arrived in Cambridge, I knew I wanted to do more, maintain my connection to the military, and serve my community however I could. My first week on campus, I went to the Commanding Officers of the two ROTC units on each side of the Charles River, at Boston University and MIT, introduced myself to them, and told them I wanted to help in any way they could use me.

Before they could formulate any specific requests, I offered one place to start. I told them that I would be starting my workouts at the base of a footbridge along the Charles River every Friday morning at six a.m., and I would open my workout to any ROTC midshipman—the Naval role designation for ROTC trainees—who wanted to join me. Initially, there was some buzz about that—a real, active-duty SEAL willing to train with them. Each of those first few Fridays, I had thirty or forty students show up. I have to admit that I was crushing them at the beginning, putting them through true SEAL workouts. It wasn't just sit-ups and push-ups—it was sprints through the Harvard football stadium, up and down the fifty stairs across the thirty-five sections of seating, knocking out twenty push-ups at the top and bottom of each section. Those were great workouts even for me—and nearly impossible for most of the students at first.

The group dwindled over time to about ten regulars, who showed up, got stronger, and started beating me—at each event, there was at least one person who ended up able to do better than I could, run or swim faster than me, do more pull-ups, push-ups, or sit-ups. On the one hand, it was awful—I can't hide my competitive nature, and there I was, an active-duty SEAL being outperformed by a bunch of college kids—but on the other hand, it was beautiful, these ten college students making me so proud and, at the same time, making me better.

This is exactly what they should have been doing, and what the SEAL environment is all about. Their performance pushed me just as I was pushing them. Now I often run by myself, and it isn't the same—me against my watch is never going to be as motivating as competing against others trying their very best.

After a year and a half of these workouts, getting to know these students well, I recommended three of them for SEAL training. After one particularly grueling Friday session, I remember intentionally finishing our run at the sidewalk in front of my house. I brought the three students into my Putnam Avenue kitchen, sat them down, and told them what it was really like to be a SEAL officer. I shared what I realize now was the beginnings of the "Never Enough" ethos, trying to figure out the lessons and wisdom I wished I'd had when I was in their shoes.

I wrote letters of recommendation for each of them, and all three got accepted. Even better, all three made it through training and went on to become SEALs. One of them, Dan, injured his leg during BUD/S training. While I was on a trip to the West Coast, one of the first things I did was stop in to check on him while he was recovering. He was doing great, and went right back into training once he was healed.

Dan ended up being incredibly successful as a SEAL. At one point during my time in Afghanistan in 2012, I had to fly from my base in Tarin Kowt over to Kandahar to visit a SEAL platoon that wasn't under my command. As the senior SEAL in Afghanistan at the time, running operations in the eastern part of the country, I would sometimes check in on the two SEAL platoons in the south, which were under Army leadership, and the one in the west, which was being led by the Marines. Dan's home station was in the west, but unbeknownst to me, he was visiting the platoons in the south at the same time as I was flying in. When I got off the plane, Dan was there on the tarmac. He had heard that I was coming, so he delayed his return to his home base—he said he couldn't miss the opportunity to say hello.

I was deeply moved. This kid who'd started showing up for my grueling six a.m. workouts less than a decade earlier was now a successful, rising officer, providing leadership in combat in Afghanistan. I was proud to think I'd made an impact on his journey.

Not long after that, Dan and a couple of his teammates were blown up by a landmine on a direct-action mission. Dan was badly wounded. I remember calling his father, explaining that I was in Afghanistan with his son, and telling him that we were going to make sure he had the best care possible. Dan ended up medically retired, blind in one eye and his vision affected in the other. He followed my path to the Harvard Kennedy School, and applied to be a White House Fellow. He made it to the final round, but ultimately didn't get chosen.

When he called to tell me he hadn't been picked as a Fellow, I gave him the advice I gave here in chapter 7: we never know how life is going to unfold, so all we can do is make the best decisions for growth at every juncture. Three months later, Dan announced a run for Congress, and as of this writing, Congressman Dan Crenshaw represents Texas's Second Congressional District. Just as I hoped to have an impact on his journey, Dan's choices in life have always extended in the direction of having an impact on as many people as he can. Though his career has unfolded in an unexpected way, overcoming obstacles at every turn, he's been motivated to serve not only the people in his community, but his country and the world.

+ + +

In the final chapter, we'll move beyond ourselves and our teams and look at how we can contribute to the world. Of course we all do that every day, with the big and little actions we take—but when we intentionally look for opportunities to make a difference, to contribute to causes that matter to us, and to push our values out to the world, especially through the people we are closest to, that's when we can really find ourselves becoming "Never Enough" in all aspects of our lives.

CHAPTER 9

MAKE DIFFERENCES WHERE THEY WILL COUNT THE MOST

Meaning in Contribution to the World

I have to start this final chapter with the story of my friend Kyle. Kyle and I were on two deployments together with SEAL Team TEN, and his love for everything Boston made us fast friends. Our bond only got stronger over the years. When I think of Kyle, I think of his character, his competence, his larger-than-life personality, and I think of Fallujah Surgical, the hospital on Camp Fallujah, our base in Iraq, the first level of care for anyone wounded in the field.

Fallujah Surgical was often a grim place. When there wasn't enough blood in the blood banks to treat wounded American troops, Camp Fallujah's loudspeaker would screech: "Anyone with A-positive blood, report immediately to Fallujah Surgical." On the worst days, the loudspeaker would call for multiple blood types at once. There isn't anything much worse than imagining a dying man or woman not having the blood they need to stay alive while you walk around with excess available to give.

One morning, early in the deployment, we finished our operation, returned to our base camp, and finally got to sleep around four in the morning. These were long, exhausting operations. We were beat. What seemed like just a moment later, we all heard the call. The loudspeaker was crying for blood.

In those moments, you want nothing more than to stay under the covers, hiding in bed, hoping and praying that someone else will hear the call first, get up, and go. You tell yourself that sleep is critical—that SEALs need their sleep to maintain operational readiness, that you're hurting the team if you don't sleep, that the consequences outweigh the benefits of waking yourself up and trudging to the hospital to sit there with a needle in your arm.

But deep down you know you're just making excuses. The consequences for you—a little less sleep—don't come anywhere close to matching the consequences for the wounded soldier who desperately needs your blood. You tell yourself that others will give—and you're probably right. But what if there aren't as many people as you think on the base that night? What if no one goes? It's a collective action problem. What if everyone decides to hide under the blankets in the hopes that someone else will step up?

I hadn't gone out on the operation the night before this particular call, so I was only one day's worth of exhausted. This made me relatively well-rested compared to some of my teammates, like Kyle, who were going out on operations every night and riding streaks of poor sleep for days. As soon as I heard the call, I forced myself up and hurried into one of our trucks to rush to the trauma center. I ignored the speed limits—the roads are quiet at four a.m.—and as I arrived, I saw the medical chaos and urgent activity all around me.

I walked into the blood bank, and there was Kyle, already sitting there with a needle in his arm. Somehow, despite days of little, if any, sleep, he had beaten me there by enough time to already be hooked up. I'll never forget the look we shared as we nodded to each other—*I'm tired, this sucks, but I'm here*, his face seemed to say, without having to speak a word out loud. Frankly, we were both too tired to talk. Kyle, whose compassion ran so deep, didn't just give blood that night. He gave life.

When I think about Kyle, I think about someone who gave life to all of us every day out there, from his practical jokes—like convincing one of our more image-obsessed teammates that he was being considered for the cover of *Men's Health* magazine and needed to impress the visiting photographer during his work-out—to the way he constantly brought new ideas to the team about things we could do better. On difficult operations, during mission planning, or simply off-duty back at headquarters, he was the first to step up no matter what the task, the first to lighten the mood with a joke or a smile, the first to look to make a difference.

Kyle was deployed for ten years straight. On his last deployment, to Somalia in 2017, he was so excited to finish up and return home, to spend more time with his wife, Erin, and their kids. He loved them with the same kind of overflowing passion with which he loved being a SEAL. He had just been accepted to the College of William & Mary to get his MBA—I had written him a tremendous letter of recommendation, because there couldn't have been a better, more committed, more capable person to do just about anything Kyle might have wanted to do in life—and he was set to start classes just a few weeks after coming home.

Tragically, devastatingly, Kyle was shot and killed on that last deployment, on a raid while he was serving as an adviser to local Somali forces pursuing radical terrorists. I was stunned when I heard the news, and broke down in tears. The world lost an amazing SEAL, an amazing hero, an amazing person.

At Kyle's memorial, I spoke about three things that I knew he understood about the life he had chosen, and that he would have wanted everyone whose lives he had touched to understand as well.

First, he would want everyone to know that he believed so strongly that the actions of the SEALs and of our military as a whole were keeping us so much safer than we would have otherwise been. He knew that putting pressure on terror networks, pursuing them and trying to knock them out, was going to limit how far they could advance and the damage they could do in the world. He knew that his work was keeping them contained as much as possible, and keeping our nation safe. He knew that this was his mission in life, and he felt strongly about the impact he was making on the world.

Second, he would want everyone to realize how important it is to contribute and fight, whether in our armed forces or outside it. He was the poster child for the "Never Enough" attitude, constantly pushing everyone on his team to get better every day, cheering them on with his quick wit and sardonic tone, supporting them however he could. When I talked to Kyle about why he wanted to go to business school, I realized that his ambitions and his model of how we can all impact the world weren't limited to the SEALs. He understood and recognized how our nation not only needs great SEALs, but also great teachers, doctors, bankers, lawyers, parents, and everyone else who makes this country strong. He realized that we all have to do what our gifts and passions push us toward.

Third, Kyle would tell everyone to give and to love as much as they can. He tried so hard to build up the people around him, to do the hard thing when no one was looking, and to treat everyone around him with the utmost respect. Kyle never missed an opportunity to help a friend or a teammate in need.

✦ ✦ ✦

I think about Kyle almost every day and try my very best to live up to the example he set. I thought about Kyle when I started writing this book, and I wondered if "Never Enough" was the right way to characterize the mindset with which I've tried to live my life, and with which Kyle certainly lived his. Was it too negative to imply that we could never be enough, do enough, invest enough of ourselves? I don't think so. I think we can simultaneously recognize how much we accomplish each day and also understand that our work is never done. There is always growth possible for each of us, ways we can push ourselves to be more excellent, more agile, and infuse our day-to-day with more meaning. There are always more people whose lives we can touch, more people we can lift up and inspire to get better and reach greater heights. It's easy to be complacent. It's harder to keep on figuring out the work we need to do. But that work is what drives us to our greatest heights. That work is what drives us to make a real contribution to the world—and the truth is that we all want to contribute, because that's what makes any of us feel fulfilled.

+ + +

In seventh grade, when my father was deployed overseas, my family lived in the US territory of Guam. Guam was a fascinating place to spend a couple of years growing up. There were about a hundred thousand civilians in Guam, and ten thousand US military—so I was very much a minority in a place with a very different culture and history, and was often the only Caucasian kid in my class. I won the science fair for my age group, and got to go to the governor's mansion, one of about twenty-five kids whose projects had been chosen. I met the governor's wife, and she gave an inspiring speech about the importance of education.

Fast-forward more than twenty-five years, and during my time in the White House, I was part of a group doing policy work related to President Obama's first trip outside the continental US. He was heading to Indonesia, and the plane would be stopping over in Guam to refuel. The reason for the stop was the fuel, but it became an opportunity to make an appearance in a US territory that is often overlooked. I was part of the team figuring out what the President could announce—some infrastructure investments—that Guam's citizens would be excited about and that would make the stopover a political success.

During this process, I ended up at a party at the White House—a screening of the Tom Hanks HBO miniseries *The Pacific*—where one of the other guests looked so familiar to me. Then I realized who she was—Madeleine Bordallo, Guam's congressional representative, and the wife of its former governor. I approached her and asked if her husband had been the governor of Guam in the mid-eighties. She told me that he had passed away, but yes indeed, he had been the governor back then. She wondered why I asked, and I told her that I had been to her house about twenty-five years earlier, in 1983, and that she had handed me a certificate recognizing my performance in the island's science fair.

She was quiet, and then I saw her eyes moisten with emotion. She softly said that in those moments, handing out those certificates, she always wondered where the children would end up and what they would do with their lives. She always wondered if they would ever make a contribution back to Guam. And here I was, she said, working in the White House, helping to make the most of the President's visit.

+ + +

It was a reminder that we all want to find meaning in what we do, and that we all want to know the things we do make a difference. It was easy to feel that—justified or not—when I was a SEAL. We execute critical, lifesaving missions; we accomplish tangible things almost every day. It's harder now in the business world, where time lines are longer and victories often more subtle. I suspect it's hard for many of us to figure out exactly how we are contributing in our lives today, and how we can best contribute going forward.

I look back a year, or three years, or ten years, and I am confident that I am so much stronger than I was before—not physically, but mentally, as far as my attitude and my understanding of the world. I know where the highest meaning is, what truly counts as contribution, how to better the lives of others, how to wake up in the morning feeling proud of what you do. I know what energizes me, what brings out the passion in my voice, the power of a network, the exponential growth of the investments we make in people, in causes, and in ourselves.

I don't have it all figured out, but I do have one final story about impact and meaning, and I think it's the perfect place to end this book. It's about my daughter, and my proudest day as a parent, bar none. My daughter has spent the past few summers volunteering in countries around the world, taking part in programs for young people aiming to pursue careers in medicine. She has spent time in clinics and orphanages, in small villages and local hospitals, shadowing doctors and nurses and helping to provide whatever care she can. In the summer of 2019, before her senior year of high school, she was in the Dominican Republic, and she called me late one morning.

"Hey, Dad," she said. "I just finished my shift in the hospital, and I saw the saddest thing." I could hear it in her voice. You never want to imagine your child in emotional pain; you just want to protect them as much as you can. But then, of course, they grow up, and you can't. "There was a woman who gave birth to a stillborn baby," she continued, "but the saddest part was that the doctor took the baby and threw it in the trash."

I sat down and swallowed hard. "It felt so wrong," my daughter said. "I couldn't bear that the mother wouldn't ever get to see the baby, to have closure, to mourn. I looked around for whatever I could find—I put on a pair of gloves, and I grabbed a cardboard box. I made the box into a little mini casket, and I took the baby out of the trash, put it in the box, cleaned it up as best as I could, and I went back into the mother's room, and in my best Spanish I told her how sorry I was, and gave the mother her baby. I held her hand, and together we cried."

I was crying, too, by the end of that, and felt so proud of the daughter my wife and I had raised, who was willing to act, to do something she felt was right, in the service of someone else who needed her. We talked about it some more, and I told her how proud I was of her; then we said goodbye. When the phone rang once more early that evening, I wasn't surprised that she was calling again. I figured this was going to take some time for her to process, and that she wanted to talk about it some more.

I was wrong. This time, her voice was racing, and I could sense the adrenaline. "Something else happened this afternoon," she said. "Fifteen of us, everyone in our program, we all went out to the beach and took a snorkeling boat out in the ocean. I was on the boat, and a bunch of the other girls were snorkeling together and having fun. But then I saw, way off to the other side, one girl was separated, alone, about 150 feet away from the group and flailing her arms. I saw her go under—and I wasn't sure anyone else had seen. I didn't have time to think. I dove off the boat, sprint-swam over to her, saw her about eight feet under, lifeless, and dove under the water. I grabbed her, pulled her up to the surface, tucked my hip under her back, and got her head out of the water. She started spitting up water, I helped clear her airway, made sure she was breathing, told her over and over that she was okay, and swam her back to the boat."

"You saved her life," I said.

"I did, Dad."

Of course, as the daughter of a Navy SEAL, she'd been comfortable in the water since she was a baby. I used to play dead in the pool and make her pull me around, and we did all kinds of exercises to make her safe and skilled in water—but to have the presence of mind to save someone like that, especially on a day when her head would have been filled with the emotions of what had happened earlier . . . well, my wife and I went to sleep that night so proud that we'd raised someone so agile, so capable of knowing the right thing to do and of actually doing it. She had always been our baby, of course, but that's when I knew that she was truly ready for the world, ready to thrive, able to understand how to live a life that's "Never Enough."

+ + +

Excellence. Agility. Meaning. I said in the Introduction that those were the critical elements, and I hope by this point you can see that, too. We can all keep striving to be the best we can be across those dimensions and so many others. We can all achieve the outcomes we are aiming for, and inspire others to achieve their goals as well. We can all serve, whether that service is as a SEAL, in politics, in the business world, for our families, or, inevitably, in a combination of all the spheres in which we work and live. We can all do our part, and understand that we are never finished. There is always more we can do for others, for ourselves, and for the world. There is *Never Enough*.

ACKNOWLEDGMENTS

First, to Ni. Thank you for your love, support, guidance, wisdom, and humor. You are the model wife and military spouse and have endured far more than I have. I will always love you more than you can imagine. It's simple: without you, this book wouldn't exist.

Maeson. You will always be my little girl. I love you with all my heart. You have always been brave, wise, and inspirational far beyond your years. I've already seen your infinite ability to positively impact the world, and you are a huge part of this book. DLY. SAP. HW.

To my parents, Ted and Elizabeth Hayes. This book is a reflection of the values, character, and work ethic you instilled and inspired in me from my earliest days. Thank you for being you, for your lifelong unwavering support, and for all you have given me.

To my siblings, Jen, John, and Maryclare. Thank you for tolerating my big brotherly and unsolicited advice. You taught me leadership, communication, and teamwork from the beginning. And, of course, thank you for teaching me how to expertly hide the Cap'n Crunch and Little Debbies. Without you three I would have never succeeded as a SEAL and in life.

To Bumpa. I miss you, but you live on deeply in me. Thank you for teaching me what selfless service really is. Thank you for your stories, from Pearl Harbor to flying search-and-rescue in Korea, and as Commanding Officer at Holy Cross. Thank you for your sword. Thank you for telling me not to die for my country, but to go on living for it.

To the most incredible book team in the world. First, Jeremy Blachman. Thank you for your incredible creativity, clear communication, inspiring partnership, unmatched work ethic, true agility, and just plain friendship. Anthony Mattero, thank you for being always proactive and positive, and for making me do the right thing—working with you! I can't imagine having done this without you. Jamie Raab. You're an incredible human with a rare blend of intense expertise and simultaneous tranquility. Thank you for your guidance, wisdom, and energy. Kate Childs, Rachel Chou, Randi Kramer, and Christine Mykityshyn. I'm indescribably appreciative of your help as I have navigated new terrain. You're each awesome.

To the institution of Holy Cross College. There's no way to list the many, many people from Holy Cross who have left indelible marks on me, so I simply say thank you to the institution for instilling the values of "people for others" in me and the world. Thank you for the culture of holding doors, even when moderately uncomfortable. In Hoc Signo Vinces.

To the SEAL Teams. It's impossible to thank the hundreds of SEAL friends who have challenged me, taught me, and inspired me to be better every day. Thank you for the opportunity to serve and learn with and among you.

To my fallen teammates. I miss each of you. I will never forget. I live my remaining days committed to helping your families and proliferating your values. I'm sorry and thank you. LLTB.

To you. Thank you for reading this book and supporting Gold Star families. And, more importantly, thank you for thinking about how you contribute to making our nation and world better through your own unique ambitions, goals, and talents in whatever ways make the most sense to YOU.

CELADON
BOOKS

Founded in 2017, Celadon Books, a division of
Macmillan Publishers, publishes a highly curated list
of twenty to twenty-five new titles a year. The list of
both fiction and nonfiction is eclectic and focuses
on publishing commercial and literary books and
discovering and nurturing talent.